ART OF LIGHT
GERMAN RENAISSANCE STAINED GLASS

SUSAN FOISTER

National Gallery Company, London
Distributed by Yale University Press

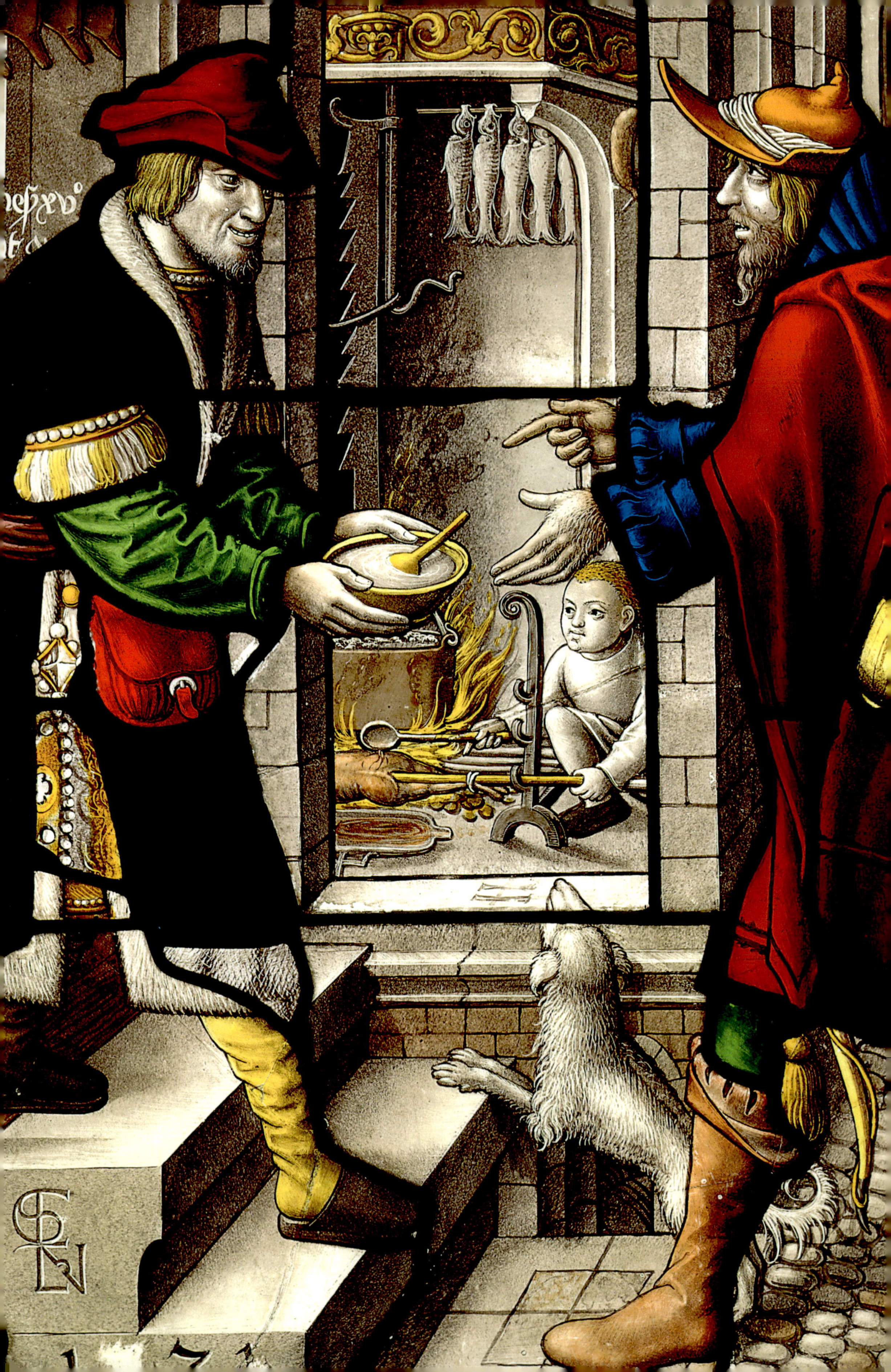

Some of the most beautiful stained glass in the history of European art was produced in Germany in the period around 1500. The use of coloured glass – so-called stained glass – in church windows had flourished from the twelfth century onwards. In Renaissance Germany much stained glass – as well as many paintings and sculpture – was made for abbeys and other ecclesiastical foundations, as well as for churches in increasingly prosperous towns such as Nuremberg, Augsburg and Cologne. By 1500 it was also found in town halls, hospitals and guildhalls, as well as in private houses and noble castles. Drawing on new secular subject matter, sometimes inspired by classical texts, as well as traditional religious themes, such glass also incorporated new, classically-inspired Renaissance motifs. Increasingly, designs for these prestigious and costly schemes were provided by the leading artists of the German Renaissance, including Albrecht Dürer, Hans Baldung Grien and Jörg Breu. Inspired with confidence in their own styles they brought fresh and individual approaches to design and colour, and to the possibilities offered as glass painting techniques became more sophisticated and varied, and the glass itself increasingly refined. The best stained glass of the period fully reflected and even rivalled the latest developments in painting, incorporating atmospheric landscape depiction and expressive and dramatic full-length figures, while exploiting to the full the vibrant properties of light.

Glass itself had been manufactured since antiquity, from a mixture of sand or crushed pebbles and an alkali (wood or plant ash), heated until it melted. By the late fifteenth century much fiercer furnaces were used and this, together with changes in the raw materials used, significantly improved the quality of the glass. It became more uniform, thinner and so more transparent. Molten glass for windows was either blown or spun, and blown cylinders of glass could be split and flattened into sheets. Glass which was spun with an iron tool formed roundels with thickened centres and these so-called 'bulls' eyes' or 'crown glass' were commonly set together to form windows in domestic settings.

German Renaissance artists of around 1500 working with either glass or panel had much in common; both were increasingly interested in creating sophisticated illusionistic effects, employing a great variety of means to achieve them, and both were adept in exploiting the properties of colour and light. Whereas glass painters were working with a naturally

Front cover:
German, detail from *Tobias and Sarah on their Wedding Night*, about 1520, glass, V&A, London

1 German, from the cloister of Mariawald Abbey, detail from *Esau gives up his Birthright*, 1521 (fig. 21c), glass, V&A, London

translucent material, panel painters used light-reflecting gold and silver leaf, matte or polished; they gave panels a brilliant white preparatory layer to increase the reflective properties of the paints and applied translucent oil glazes over opaque paint, as well as mixing pigments with white, to render the varying effects of shadows and reflected light. Panel painters did not confine themselves to working with brushes but used stamps and burnishing tools for gilding, and stencils to create patterns. The ends of their brushes could be used to make grooves in wet paint, cloth to blot a damp glaze to create a spotted effect and wet paint worked thinly or thickly to create shaded or three dimensional effects.

Glass painters used a similar range of techniques. The process of making coloured glass windows was described by the twelfth-century monk Theophilus. The colouring agents were quite different from those of the painter, which were made from minerals or earths ground to a fine consistency, or from dyes extracted from insects or plants, although German painters did sometimes use the blue pigment smalt, which was itself made from ground blue glass. For coloured glass, metal oxides or ores were heated with the glass in terracotta pots; the resulting glass is known for this reason as 'pot metal'. Cobalt produced a brilliant blue, copper could give a blue, green or red colour and manganese produced purple glass. Red glass made in this way with copper oxide is very intense in colour, so glass of the thickness usually used in a window would not let sufficient light through and would look black. A technique known as flashing was therefore developed, by which a bubble of white glass was dipped in molten coloured glass and then blown, so a thin layer of colour overlaid the white, allowing the colour to be brilliantly illuminated by light. A further refinement was to scrape away part of the coloured glass with a grinding tool, to allow a contrasting patterned effect. By 1500 a variety of colours could be produced, and even different grades of colourless glass. To make up a window, pieces of coloured glass were cut to the required shapes by first scoring with a hot iron rod and trimming with a steel-pointed tool known as a grozing iron; they were joined with H-shaped lead strips or 'cames'. The 'cames' were soldered together, giving the heavy black outlines characteristic of stained glass windows. After 1500 it became possible to use larger pieces of glass, so the leading gradually became a less important part of the design.

Glass painters in Germany had traditionally used a black or brown vitreous enamel paint, known as 'matte', 'Schwarzlot' or 'Braunlot' and fixed by firing onto the front of the glass to create dark outlines. But it could also be used in a more sophisticated and painterly manner, as a wash; working into the wash with stippling brushes or styluses, glass painters produced delicate modelling and textural effects. The use of washes to

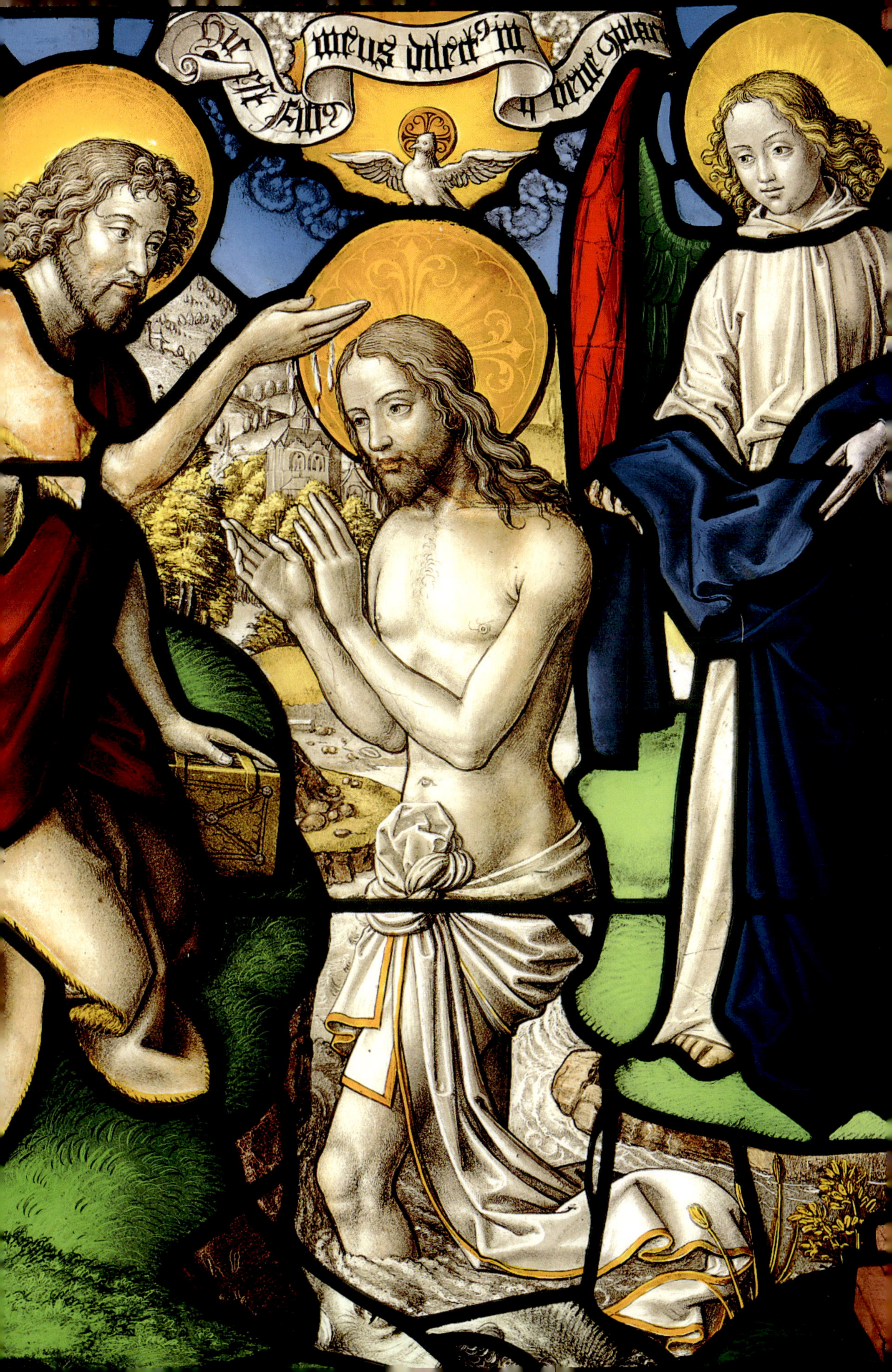
hic e̅ filius meus dilect[us] in q[u]o michi c̅plac[ui]

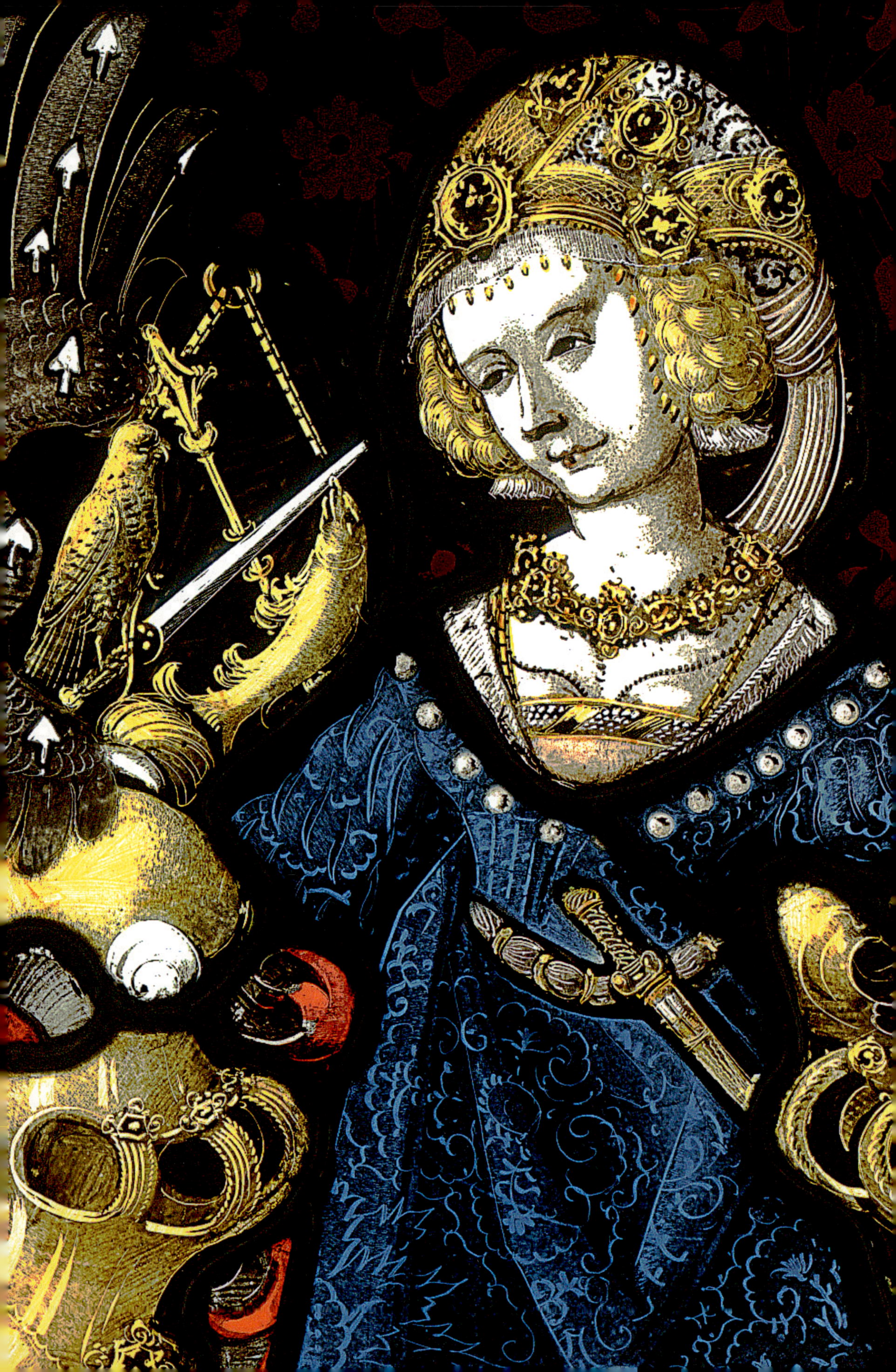

produce the most subtle shading was first seen in the great glass-making centre of Strasbourg in the second half of the fifteenth century; in the sixteenth century, new techniques now allowed far greater pictorial variety within a single piece of coloured or uncoloured glass. Glass painters experimented with obtaining varied and subtle tones and colours by differing combinations of paint composition, types of glass and lengths of firing. They were aided by better tools; as well as needles and sticks and the large 'badger' brushes used for stippling, small silver-wire brushes allowed more controlled application.

Such techniques were used to create an extraordinary range of vivid effects: deeply folded fabric, whether plain cloth or elaborate damasks, gleaming metalwork and hair, flesh and fur. The charming panel of *Tobias and Sarah on their Wedding Night* (cover) presents an episode from the Old Testament story: Sarah had 'brought death' to seven previous bridegrooms on their wedding night, but Tobias managed to avoid this fate by taking the advice of the Archangel Raphael not to consummate the marriage for three days. Thus the couple are shown in chaste slumber, their nightcap-clad heads propped against plump pillows, within a luxuriously appointed bed. The glazier has selected a teardrop shaped piece of deep red glass to represent one of the bed curtains, looped up the better to display the bed, as was usual at the time; the red glass has been worked up with the dark 'matte' to create a convincing sense of the folded curtain. On the small, oval piece of whiteish glass set into the bed cover, the artist has depicted a sleeping dog, the texture of his curling hair minutely conveyed. To the left is a table, subtly shaded to represent both its three-dimensional bulk and the grain of the wood.

Another tour-de-force is a heraldic piece by the leading Swiss glass painter Lukas Zeiner. The beautifully detailed head and bosom of the female figure are formed from a single piece of glass, decorated with great verve and subtlety, using a combination of techniques. The stitched edge and white highlights of the folded linen chemise visible at her left shoulder were created by scratching away the 'matte' to reveal pure white glass. To create the shadows of the folds in her gown, pieces of blue glass have been brushed with 'matte'; this was then scraped away, perhaps with a brush handle, to give the outlines of the damask pattern, appearing as the lightest blue. The background behind the figure is of plum coloured glass with a bolder decorative pattern, perhaps applied using a stencil.

Not all glass achieved such heights of artistic endeavour. But even simpler pieces, and those from an earlier period, display the close links that existed between glassmaking, drawing and painting.

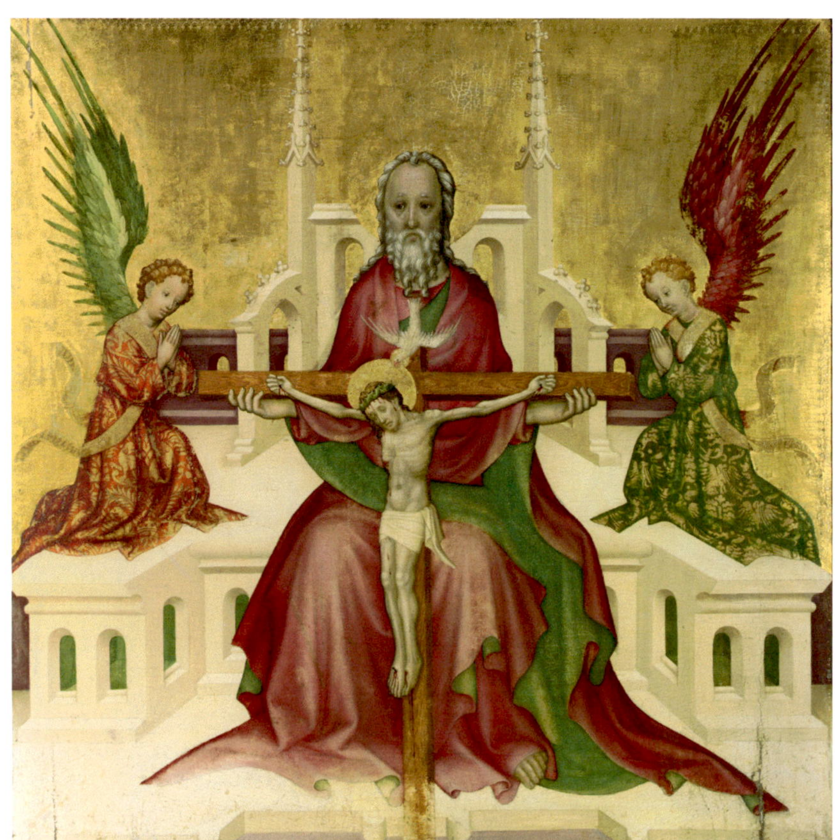

The National Gallery's painting of the *Trinity* by an unknown Austrian painter of around 1410 (fig. 4) and the glass panel depicting the *Annunciation to Saint Anne*, from Strassengel near Graz in Austria, of around 1350 (fig. 5), are strikingly similar in style, despite being made by very different methods. This is especially true of the long feathered wings of the angels, the monumentally architectural thrones and the draping of folded cloth over seated figures. The background to the glass panel is created by painting a diamond pattern onto ruby glass; the background of the painted panel is covered in gold leaf, and bordered with a stamped pattern, not unlike the circular pattern edging the glass panel. In the painting the angels' robes resemble rich gold damasks; the pattern of animals is created with transparent red and green glazes over gold leaf. Interestingly, the glass panel uses a much greater range of colours than the painting, which confines itself to a palette of red and green, though flesh, hands and faces are depicted by the glass painter in a more linear fashion, with a minimum of shading.

By 1500 a new technique which allowed a different, more painterly approach to colouring glass had become highly popular in northern Europe. This was the use of yellow silver stain. Medieval recipes specified a mixture of silver compounds mixed with red or yellow earth,

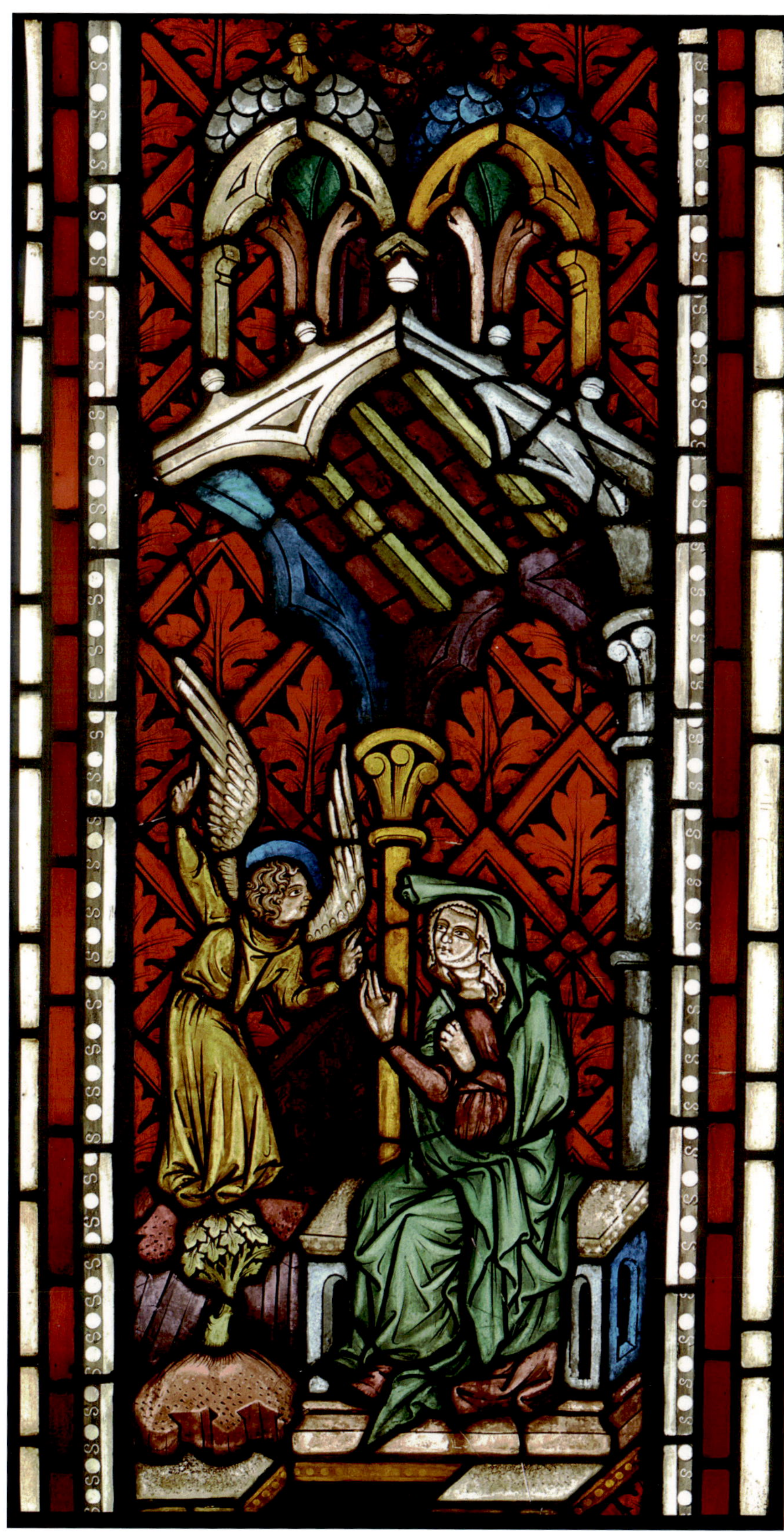

5 Austrian,
*The Annunciation
to Saint Anne*,
about 1350–5,
glass, 104 x 35.5 cm,
V&A, London

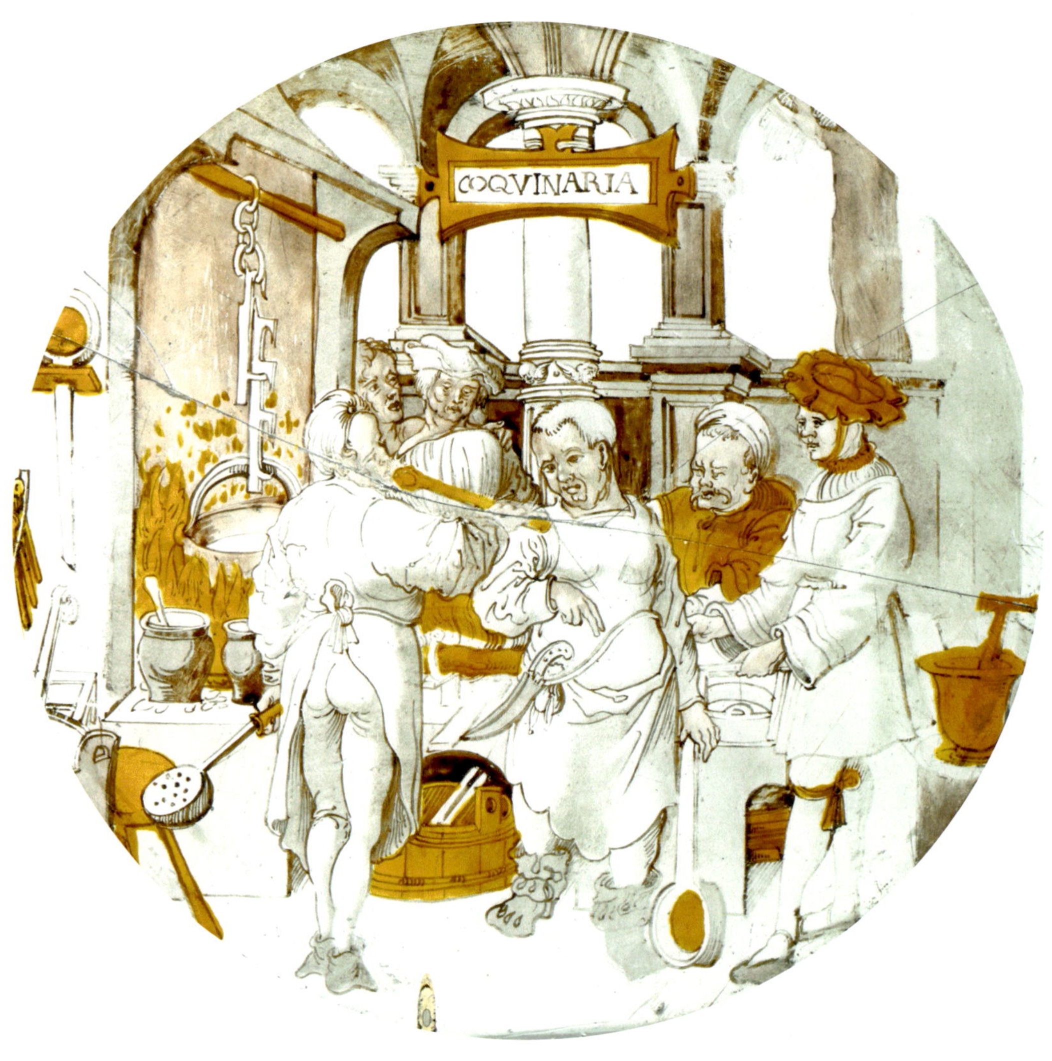

pipe clay or brick dust, which was applied with brush or spatula to the back of the glass and then fired. The silver compounds penetrated into the glass during firing, imparting a range of hues from pale lemon to egg yolk or even orange, which were revealed when the chalky residue was buffed off. Silver stain was particularly popular for small individual roundels or rectangles with otherwise monochrome designs, such as those made after designs by the Augsburg artist Jörg Breu (who also worked in Cologne) (figs 7 and 8). Usually highly wrought, using the most sophisticated techniques, they were eminently suitable for secular settings where their quality could be appreciated in close view.

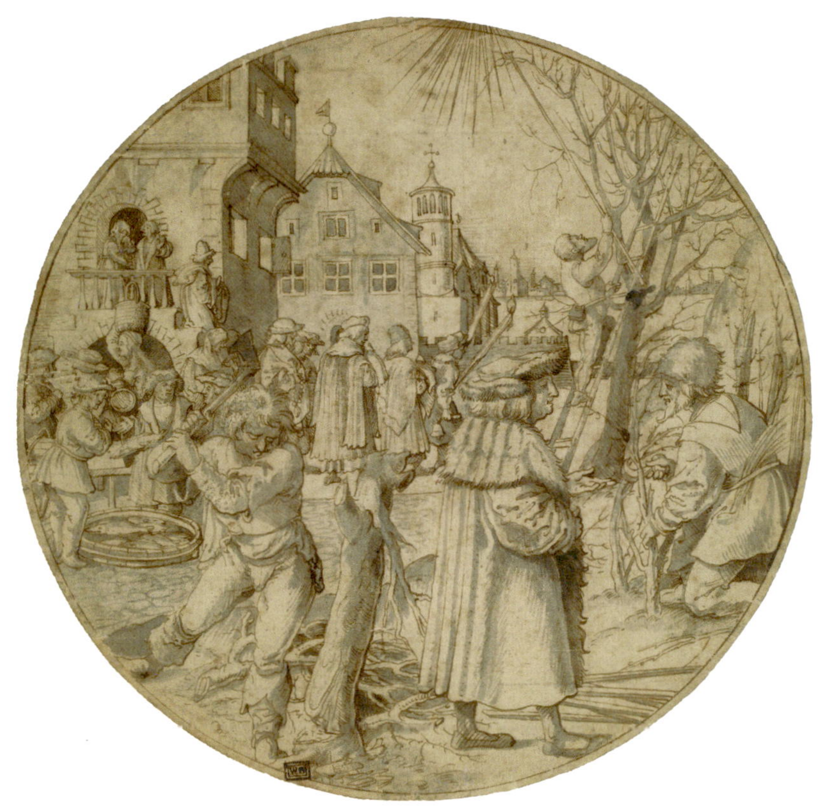

7 Jörg Breu the Elder (about 1475–1537), *March*, before 1521, pen and ink with wash on paper, 24.4 cm diameter, The British Museum, London

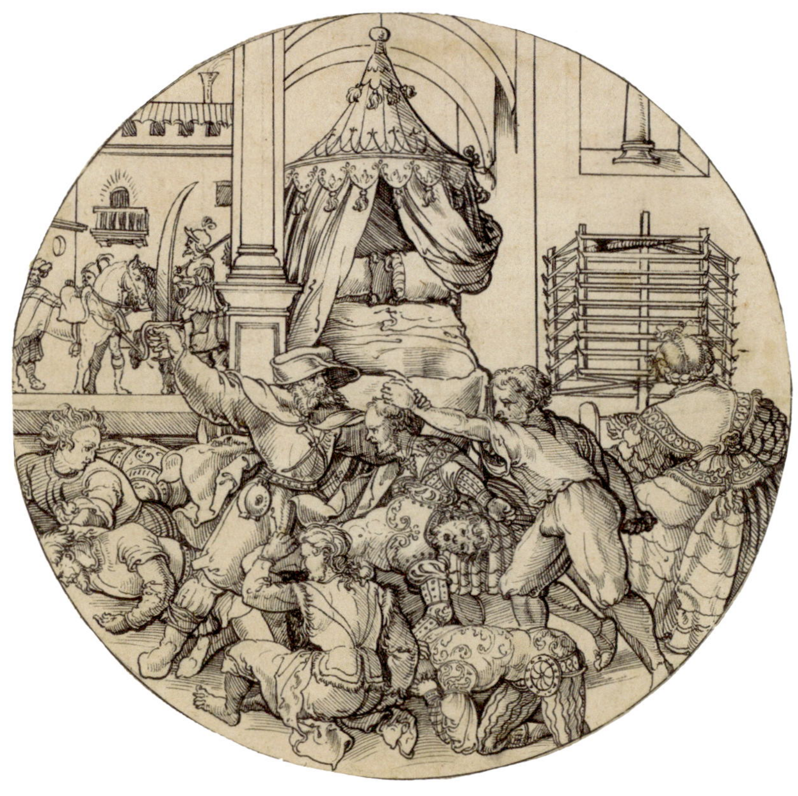

8 Jörg Breu the Elder (about 1475–1537), *Ulysses and Telemachus slaying the Suitors*, 1522, pen and ink on paper, 24.4 cm diameter, The British Museum, London

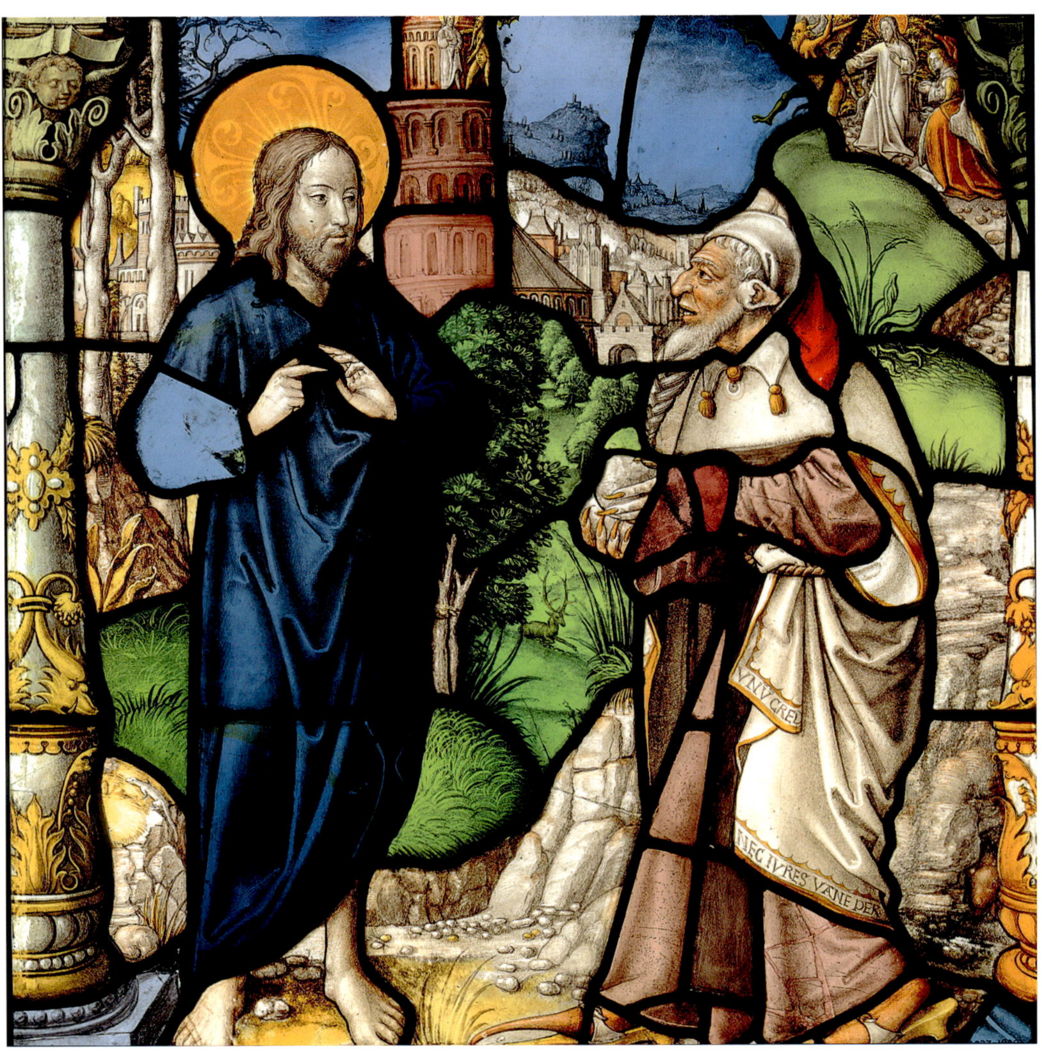

9 German, from the cloister of Mariawald Abbey, *The Temptation of Christ*, about 1520–1, glass (fig. 21e), 71.5 x 70 cm, V&A, London

Silver stain was also used in coloured glass designs. A glass painter might for example use blue glass shaded to represent sky, clouds and distant mountains, with silver stain over the blue to create a green and less distant landscape, as for example in Dürer's *Annunciation* (see fig. 14, p. 16). In the *Temptation* from the Abbey of Mariawald (fig. 9) blue glass creates both sky and distant landscape, while green is used for the middle ground, but in the atmospheric winter landscape background of *Abbot Heinrich von Binsfeld*, also from Mariawald (fig. 10), brown paint and silver stain create a shaded effect on colourless glass. Further developments in the sixteenth century brought stained glass effects even closer to painting. Brownish-red was added to the black and browns used to paint on coloured glass, and a whole range of vitreous enamel colours fixed by firing was introduced. By the end of the century painting with these colours on large colourless glass panels dominated, and the subtle balance of painterly techniques and coloured glass, at its height in Germany in the early sixteenth century, was lost.

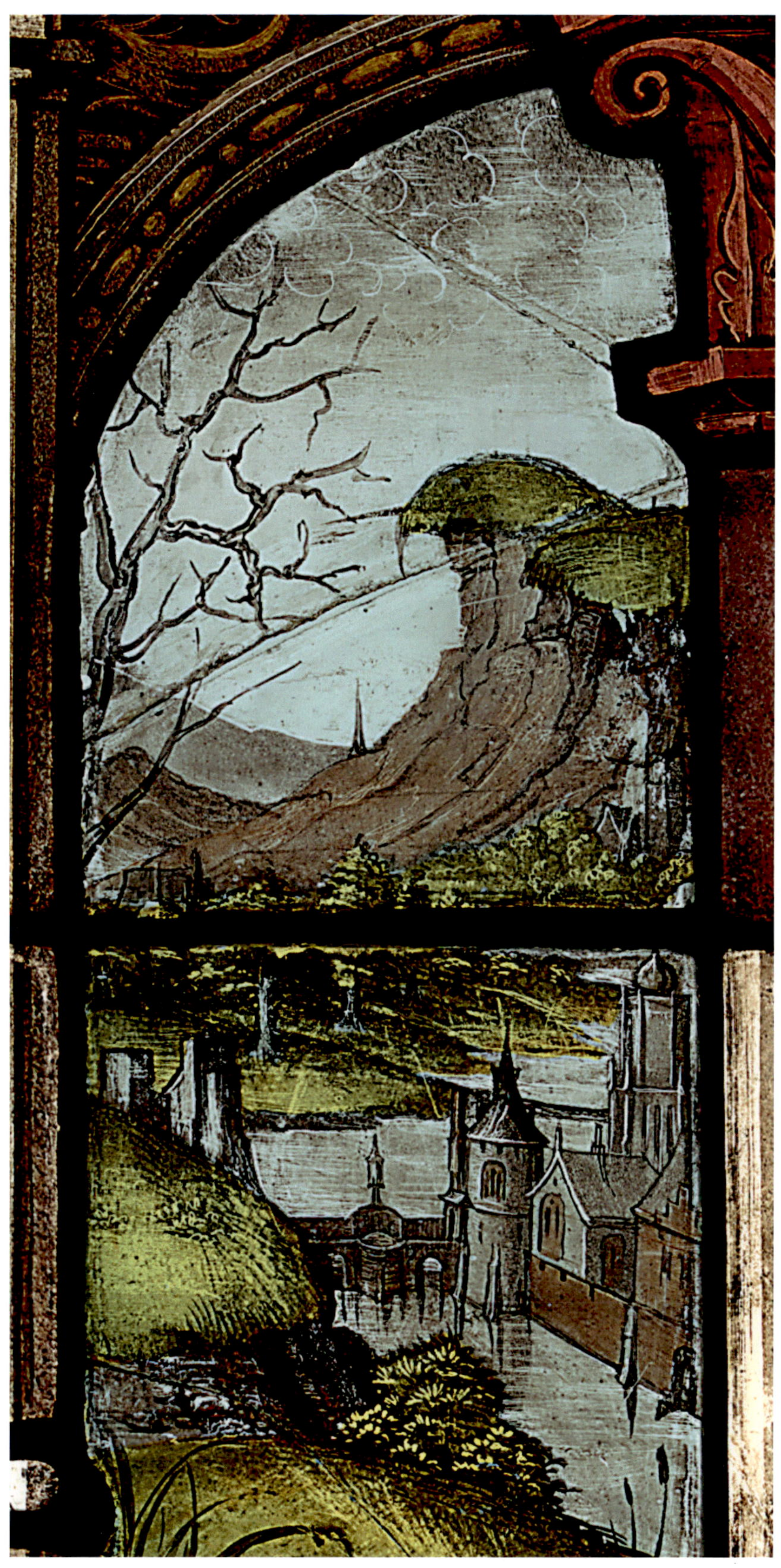

10 German, from the cloister of Mariawald Abbey, detail from *Abbot Heinrich von Binsfeld*, about 1520–1 (fig. 21h), glass, V&A, London

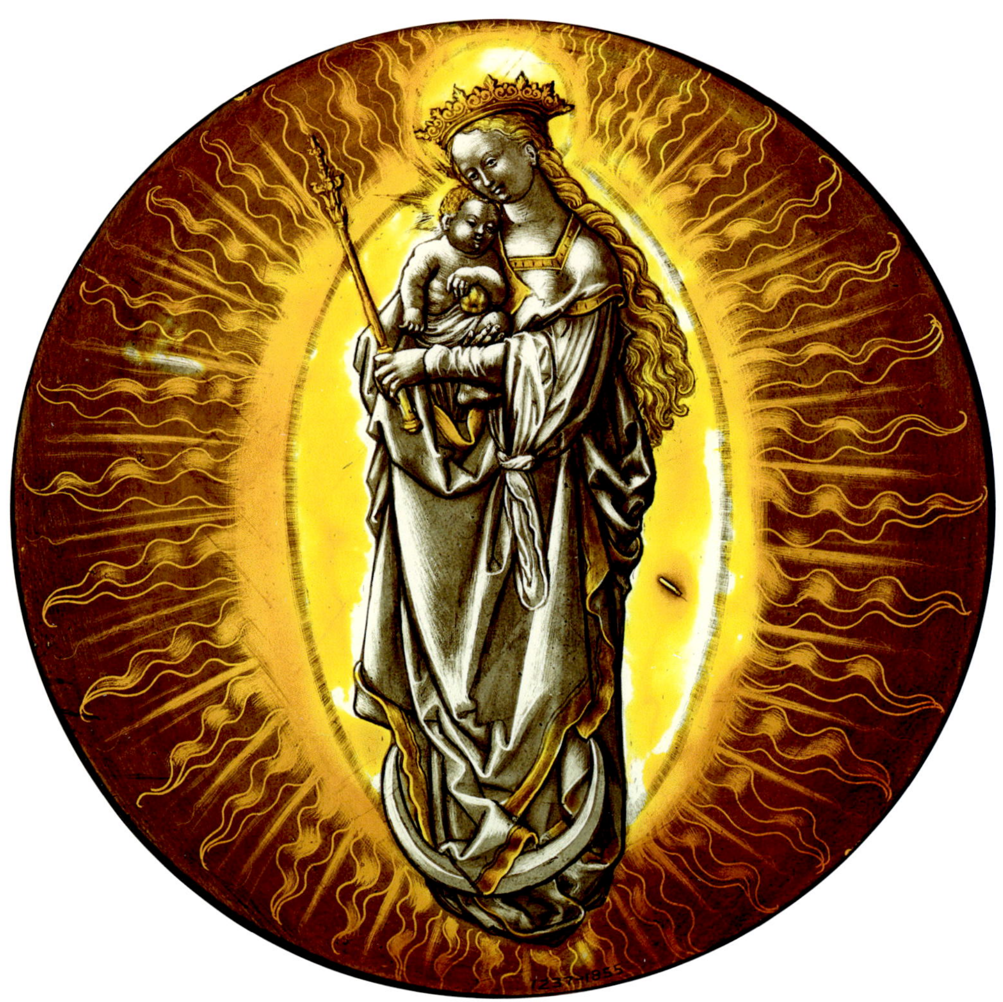

Who created the exceptional stained glass of this period? In medieval
Germany the makers of stained glass worked separately from painters,
using designs from a variety of sources. But by the early sixteenth
century painters were far more involved in creating stained glass than
before; powerful patrons wanted to reflect the visionary innovations of
leading artists, notably Albrecht Dürer in Nuremberg. Although major
artists such as Dürer did not themselves paint the glass, Dürer had a
close association with the Nuremberg glazier Veit Hirsvogel, Baldung
with Hans Gitschmann von Ropstein in Freiburg, and the Augsburg
artist Jörg Breu with Hans Braun; there is some evidence to suggest that
on occasion painters with specific glass-painting skills would be sent from
a painter's workshop to work on a commission with the glaziers.

In the medieval period, before paper was widely available, designs for
stained glass windows were usually drawn out full size on a whitewashed
table. By the end of the fifteenth century, painters would often provide
designs in the form of sketches to glazier's workshops, which could be

worked up into full-size cartoons for windows. Drawings to be approved by patrons were known as 'vidimuses', meaning 'we have seen'. They formed a record of a binding contract to deliver that design for the window.

Many designs survive by Jörg Breu, mostly for small roundels, and the popularity of these led to the making of many copies and adaptations by glassmakers, even late in the sixteenth century. *Ulysses and Telemachus* (fig. 8) shows the careful linear precision of Breu's initial drawing, probably for the patron, and too complex for direct translation into glass. It demonstrates the assurance with which he manipulated complex spatial drama within the confines of the roundel, using the vertical and horizontal axes to create strong contrasts between space and action. His drawing for *March* (fig. 7) includes wash probably put in as a guide for the glass painter once the patron had approved the first design; the glass painter would then have taken copies which could be set under the glass and traced directly onto it. Glaziers without a direct relationship with a painter could use prints as sources for glass designs: for example the small roundel of *The Virgin as Queen of Heaven* (fig. 11) is based on an engraving by Dürer, while the glass panels illustrating the Passion are based on Dürer's woodcut Passion series (figs 12 and 13).

Dürer made designs for stained glass throughout his career. In this as in other arts he was an innovator, and the legacy of his bold, imaginative designs extended throughout the sixteenth century, with his prints also a highly important source for glassmakers. Dürer's designs marked a new monumentality in the creation of stained glass, reflecting the clarity and simplicity in composition, and the interest in the ideal proportions of the human figure and in spacious landscape depiction, which animated his

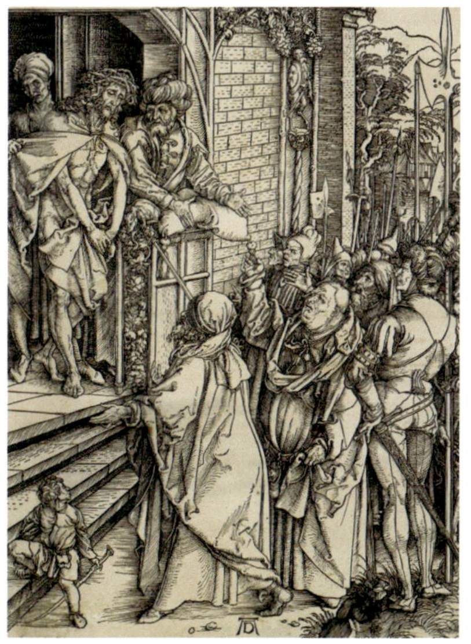

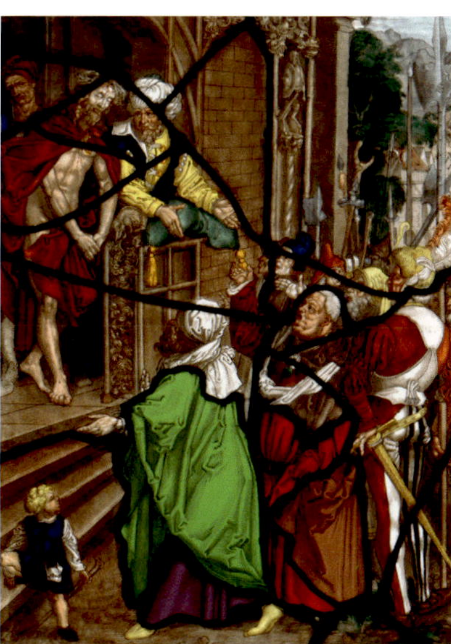

12 Albrecht Dürer (1471–1528) *Ecce Homo*, about 1497–1500, woodcut, 39.2 x 28.4 cm, The British Museum, London

13 German, after Dürer, *Ecce Homo*, mid-16th century, glass, about 64.7 x 30 cm, V&A, London

15

painting and printmaking. Members of his workshop including Baldung and Hans von Kulmbach were particularly active and prolific in creating such designs and cartoons under his supervision. The glazier Veit Hirsvogel was Dürer's most frequent and accomplished collaborator; one of their most impressive works was the glass for the Tucher Garden Chapel in Nuremberg. *The Annunciation* of about 1504–5 (fig. 14) was placed at the centre of the five-sided chapel choir, which had ten windows in all. Almost four feet high, the design shows the three-dimensionality of Dürer's figures fully rendered against a landscape seen through a window. The green damask curtain and the gold design of the Virgin's cloak mirror the effects seen in contemporary painting, while the lily of the valley in the pot at her feet recalls the beautiful plant studies that Dürer also incorporated into his paintings. By employing sophisticated techniques including a range of applications of silver stain and working with tools, hatching and scratching, Hirsvogel achieved a subtle yet highly expressive rendering of Dürer's design. No drawings survive for the commission, but it is possible Dürer made the cartoon himself.

Baldung worked with Dürer until 1509 when he returned to his native Strasbourg. Hardly any glass survives directly based on his drawings, although these are numerous. The most important of these is the design for a pair of monumental windows for a convent near Strasbourg. The drawing for one of these, of the Abbess Hohenberg (fig. 15), shows his exceptional powers of design; the rhythm of the crisply interlocked folds of the kneeling nuns contrasts with the ebullience of the foliage which dances along the upper architecture. A similarly effective interaction between donor figures and the rest of the design is evident in Baldung's *Trinity*, an altarpiece probably made for the church of St Peter the Old in Strasbourg (fig. 16).

From 1512–17 Baldung worked in Freiburg-im-Breisgau, where he painted the large and arresting altarpiece of the *Coronation of the Virgin* which remains in situ there. New windows designed by Baldung were produced for the choir in 1515/16, of which the *Man of Sorrows* and *Mater Dolorosa* survive (see figs 19 and 20). These two glass panels, for which he himself probably made the cartoons, were executed with immense skill by the workshop of Hans Gitschmann von Ropstein. Baldung's great originality is evident; the designs are exceptionally bold in their control of large expanses of red and blue, a limited palette presumably chosen by Baldung himself, and reflecting his confident painting style of this time. In contrast, the veins and bones in the legs and feet of Christ are executed in immense detail, to extraordinarily vivid effect. The modelling of the veil and the face of the Virgin with scratched out highlights, grey wash and hatching in three shades of paint captures

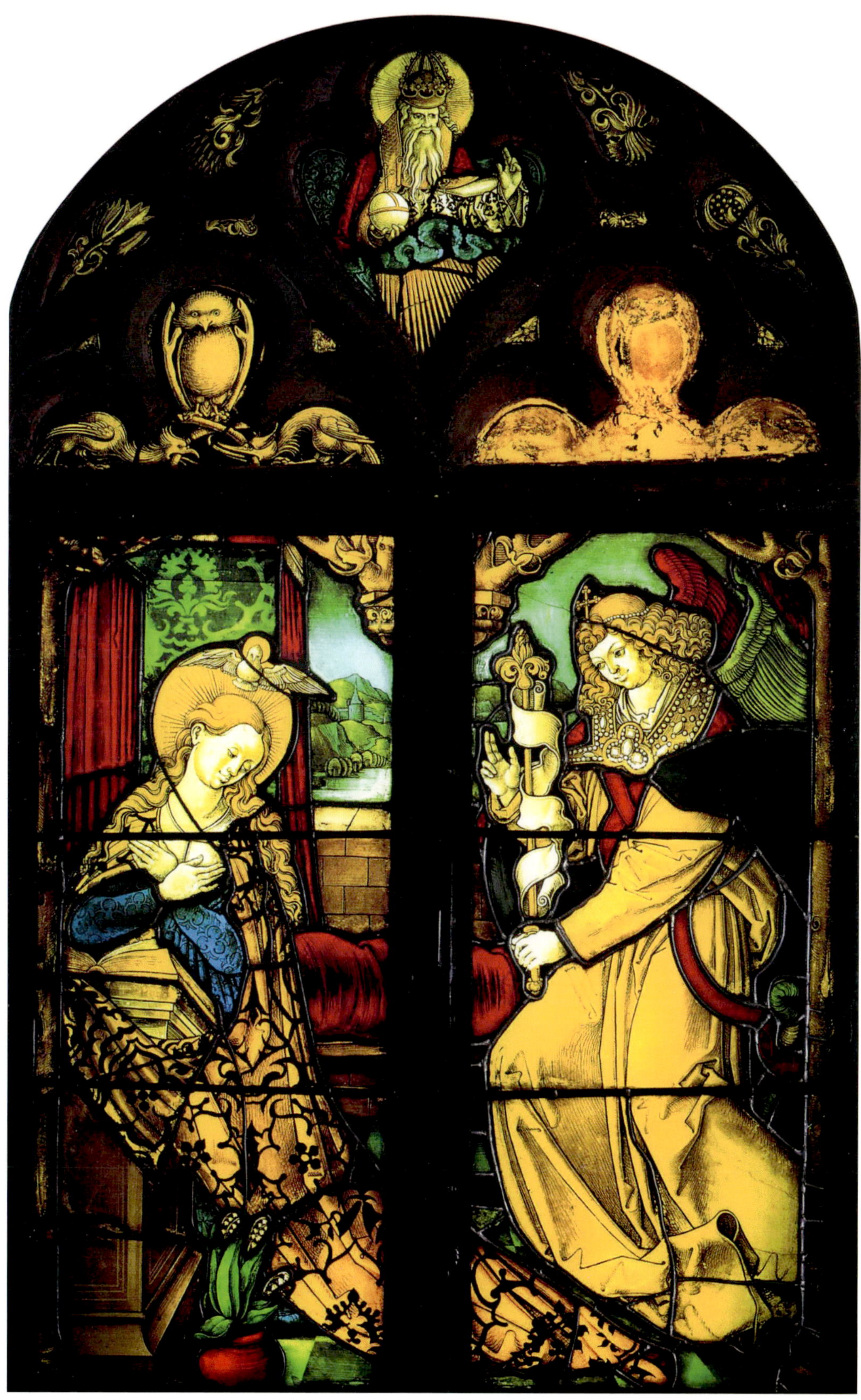

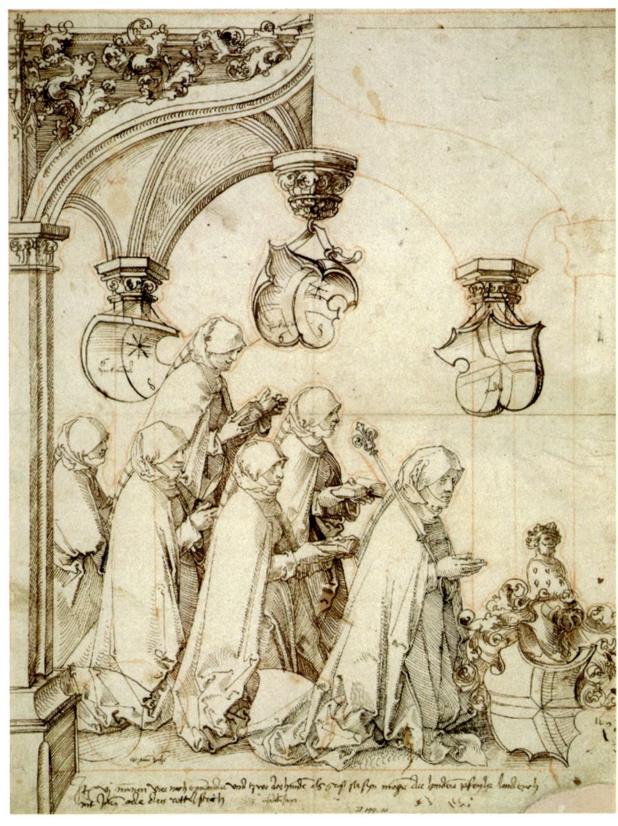

15 Hans Baldung Grien (1484/5–1545), *The Abbess Veronica von Andlau, with Nuns of Cloister Hohenburg,* about 1510, pen and brown ink on paper, 43 x 31.5 cm, V&A, London

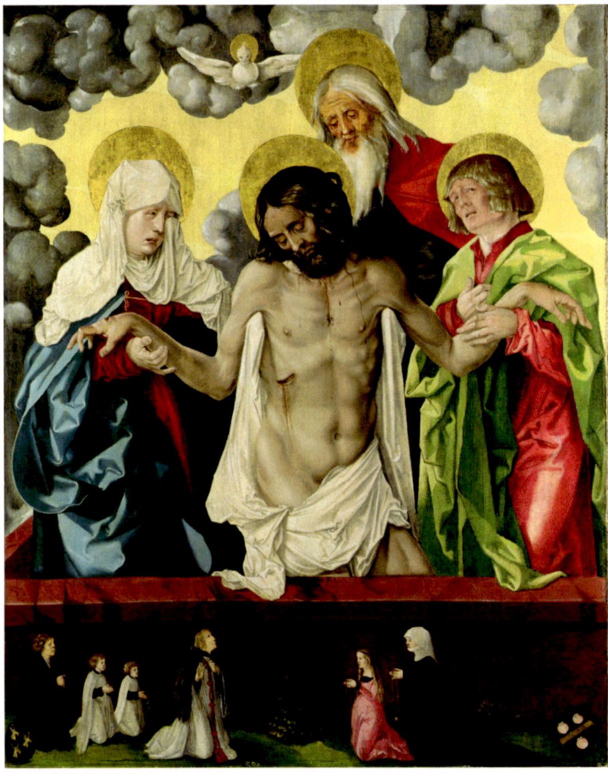

16 Hans Baldung Grien (1484/5–1545), *The Trinity and Mystic Pietà*, 1512, oil on oak, 112.3 x 89.1 cm, The National Gallery, London

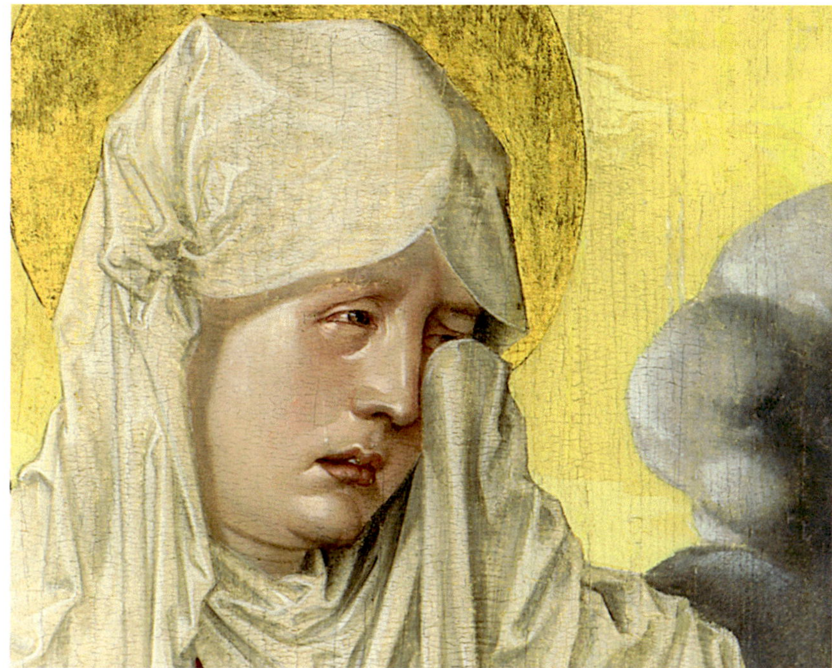

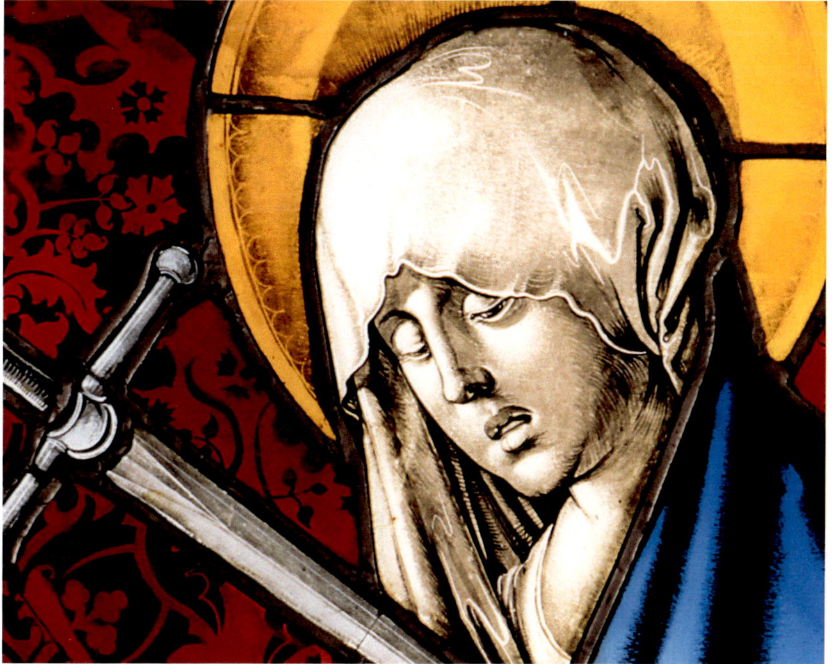

her sorrowing expression, comparable to the emotion of the weeping
Virgin in the same artist's painting of the *Trinity* (figs 16, 17 and 18).

During the middle ages, both the tall stained glass windows and the
large shuttered altarpieces of abbeys and church buildings commonly
took as their subject the Christian theme of redemption, often
juxtaposing scenes from the Old Testament with the New, so that
the former could be seen as prefiguring the latter. Some of the most

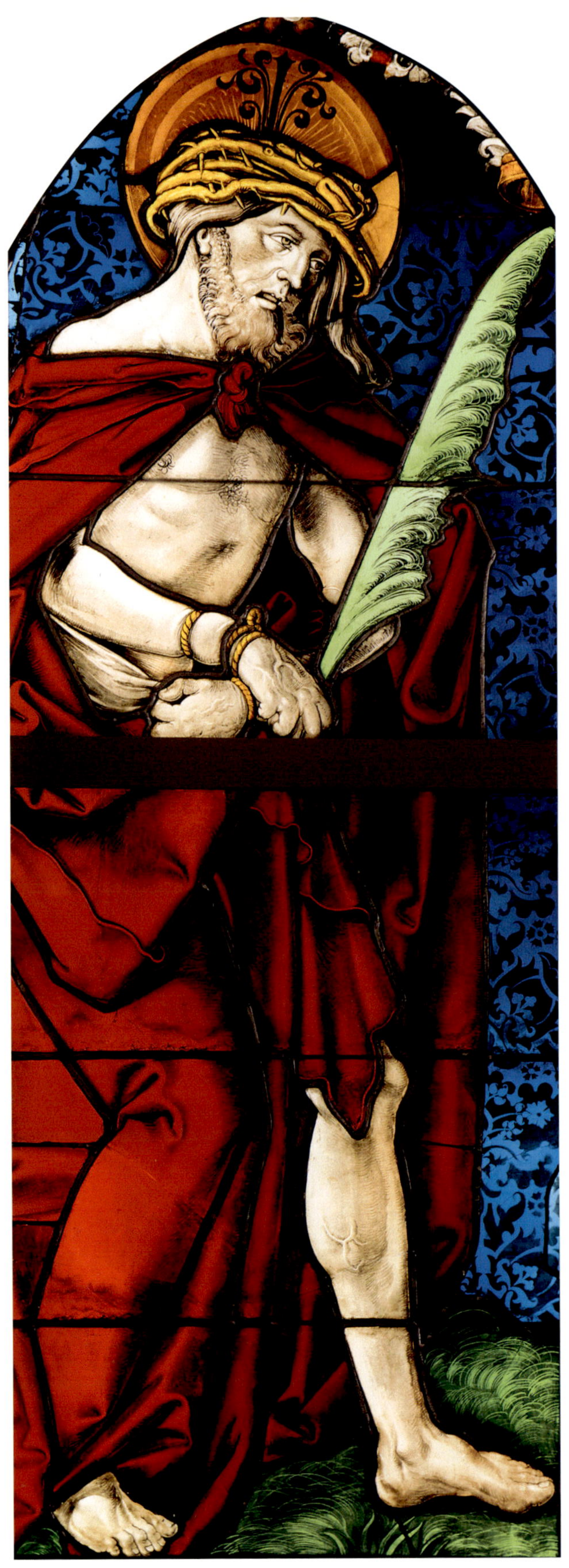

19 After Hans Baldung Grien, workshop of Hans Gitschmann von Ropstein (1480/5–1564), *Christ as the Man of Sorrows*, about 1516, glass, 147 x 52 cm, Badisches Landesmuseum Karlsruhe, Karlsruhe (C8524)

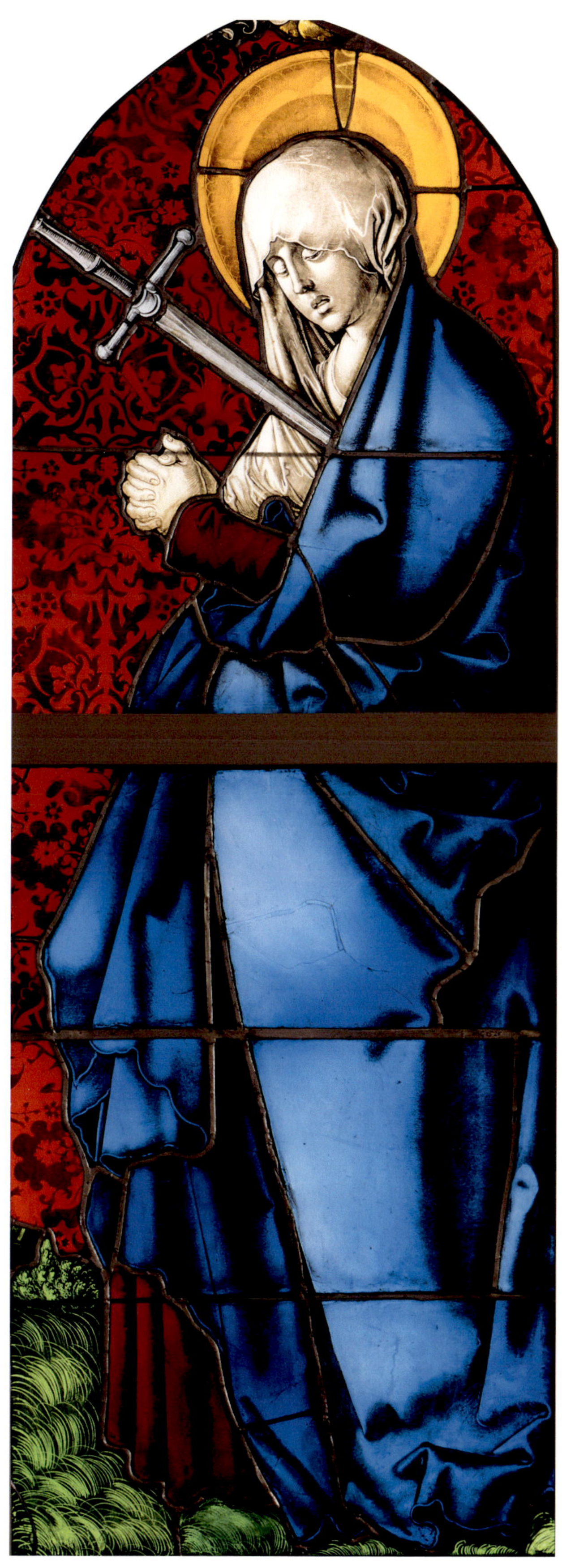

20 After Hans
Baldung Grien,
workshop of Hans
Gitschmann von
Ropstein
(1480/5–1564),
Mater Dolorosa,
about 1516,
glass, 148 x 53 cm,
Badisches Landes-
museum Karlsruhe,
Karlsruhe (C8525)

magnificent German glass from the early sixteenth century comes from the cloister of the Cistercian abbey of Mariawald in the Eifel region of the Lower Rhine, founded in 1480. The glass can be dated to the second and third decades of the sixteenth century, though some scenes follow closely engravings by Martin Schongauer, produced in the fifteenth century. The windows were arranged with prophets at the head of each 'light' and paired Old and New Testament scenes and donor panels below. A typical sequence (facing page), showing the extraordinarily high quality of the design and painting of these windows, includes the portrait of Heinrich von Binsfeld, Abbot of the imperial abbey of Cornelimünster near Aachen 1491–1531 (fig. 21h), who donated two windows to Mariawald. The panel of *Esau gives up his Birthright* (figs 1 and 21c) is dated 1521 and has a monogram which resembles that of the glazier Gerhard Remisch, though it is not identical. The Esau panel, with its vivid evocation of the stripy scales of the mackerel-like fish being smoked over the fire, was set over one of the *Temptation of Christ* (fig. 21e), setting two temptations against each other. Similarly *Naaman washing in the River Jordan* (fig. 21d) was set over the *Baptism of Christ* (fig. 21f). The donor panel (bottom right, and p. 12) includes not only spectacularly elaborate and varied examples of Renaissance decorative panels but also an atmospheric wintry landscape with bare branches and reflections of buildings in water.

These panels can be compared directly to the shutters of the Liesborn altarpiece by Jan Baegert, the Master of Cappenberg, who in 1517 added shutters of the Passion of Christ to the earlier panels of the Crucifixion and early life of Christ begun after 1470 (figs 22–4). The clarity with which the Mariawald scenes tell the Old and New Testament stories is matched in the way Baegert has composed his panels, using very similar compositional devices. In the Mariawald *Naaman* (fig. 21d) the central scene is set off by the arresting figure of a man in red hose, while in the Liesborn *Christ before Pilate* Baegert similarly introduces on the right a soldier in blue and white striped hose, who brings Christ to Pilate on his throne. The arrangement of this scene, with the central figures flanked by those in the middle distance, is also comparable to the subtly subdued *Presentation in the Temple* from the slightly earlier Mariawald series (fig. 24).

21 German, reconstruction of a window from the cloister of Mariawald Abbey. After Hans Baldung Grien, workshop of Hans Gitschmann von Ropstein (1480/5–1564). From left to right, top to bottom: a. *The Prophet David*, 33 x 67.9 cm; b. *The Prophet David*, 29.4 x 65.9 cm; c. *Esau gives up his Birthright*, 69.6 x 67.3 cm; d. *Naaman washing in the River Jordan*, 69.6 x 65.9 cm; e. *The Temptation of Christ*, 71.5 x 70 cm; f. *The Baptism of Christ*, 73.2 x 66.3 cm; g. *Saint Cornelius*, 77 x 70.5 cm; h. *Abbot Heinrich von Binsfeld of Cornelimünster*, 77 x 70.5 cm. 1520–1, glass, V&A, London.

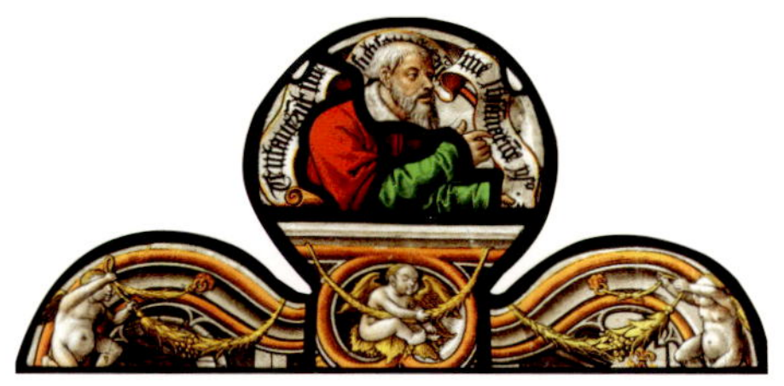

a

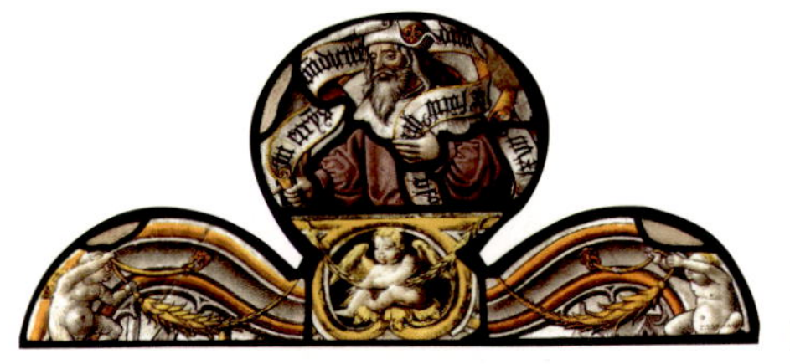

b

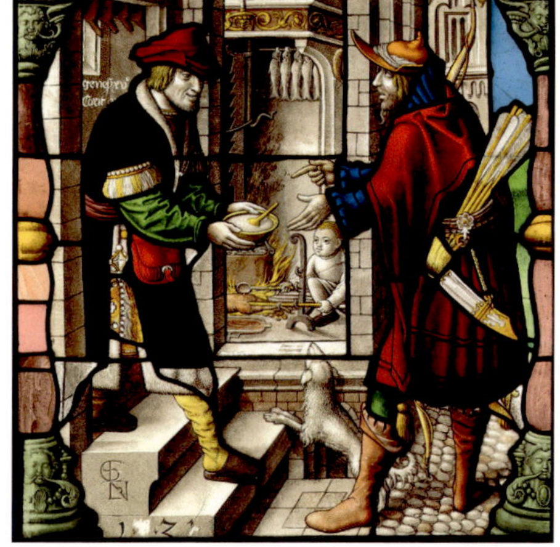

c

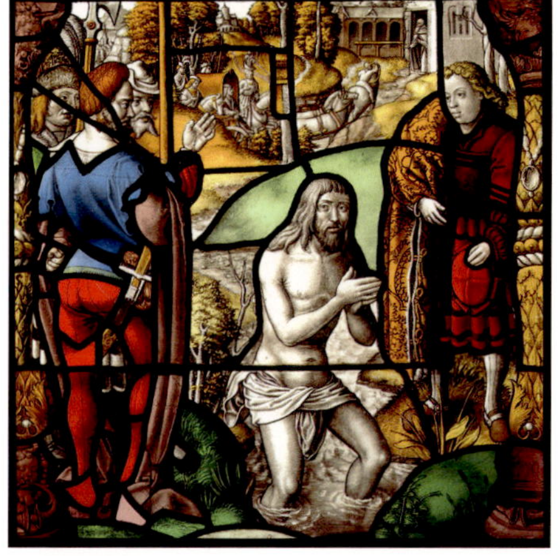

d

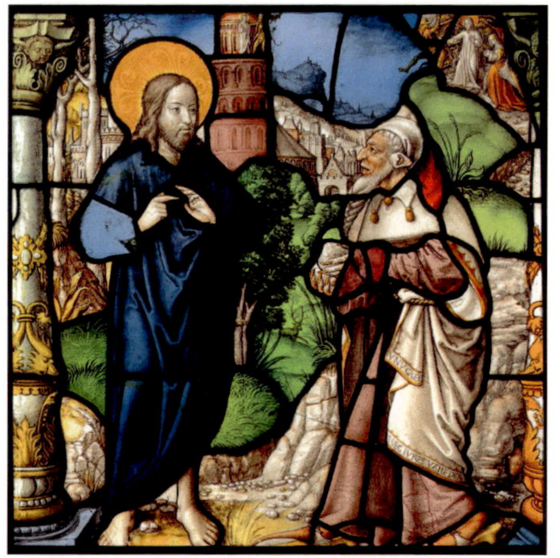

e

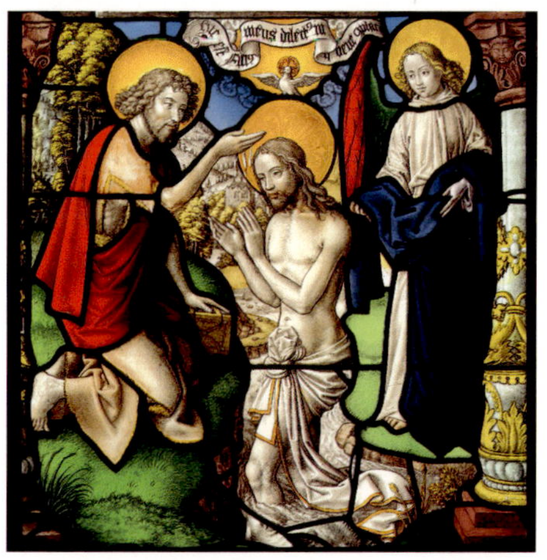

f

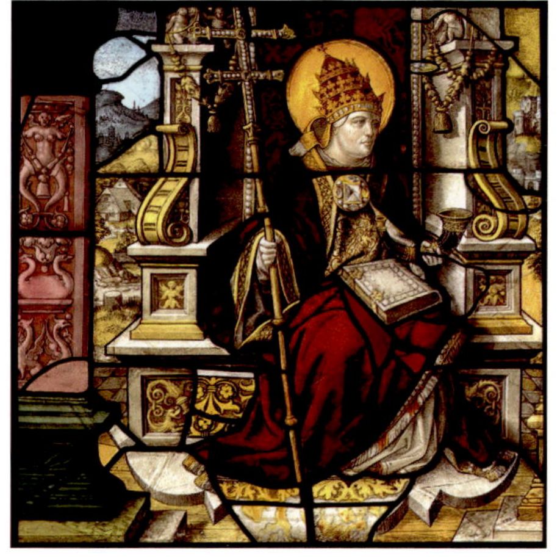

g

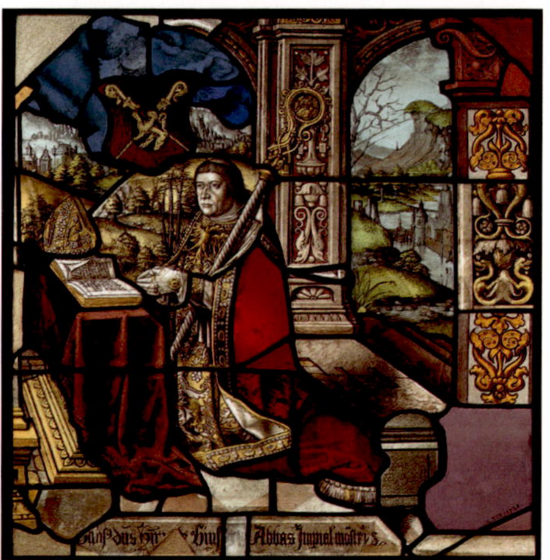

h

22 German, from the
cloister of Mariawald
Abbey, detail from
*Naaman washing
in the River Jordan*,
about 1520–1
(fig. 21d), glass,
V&A, London

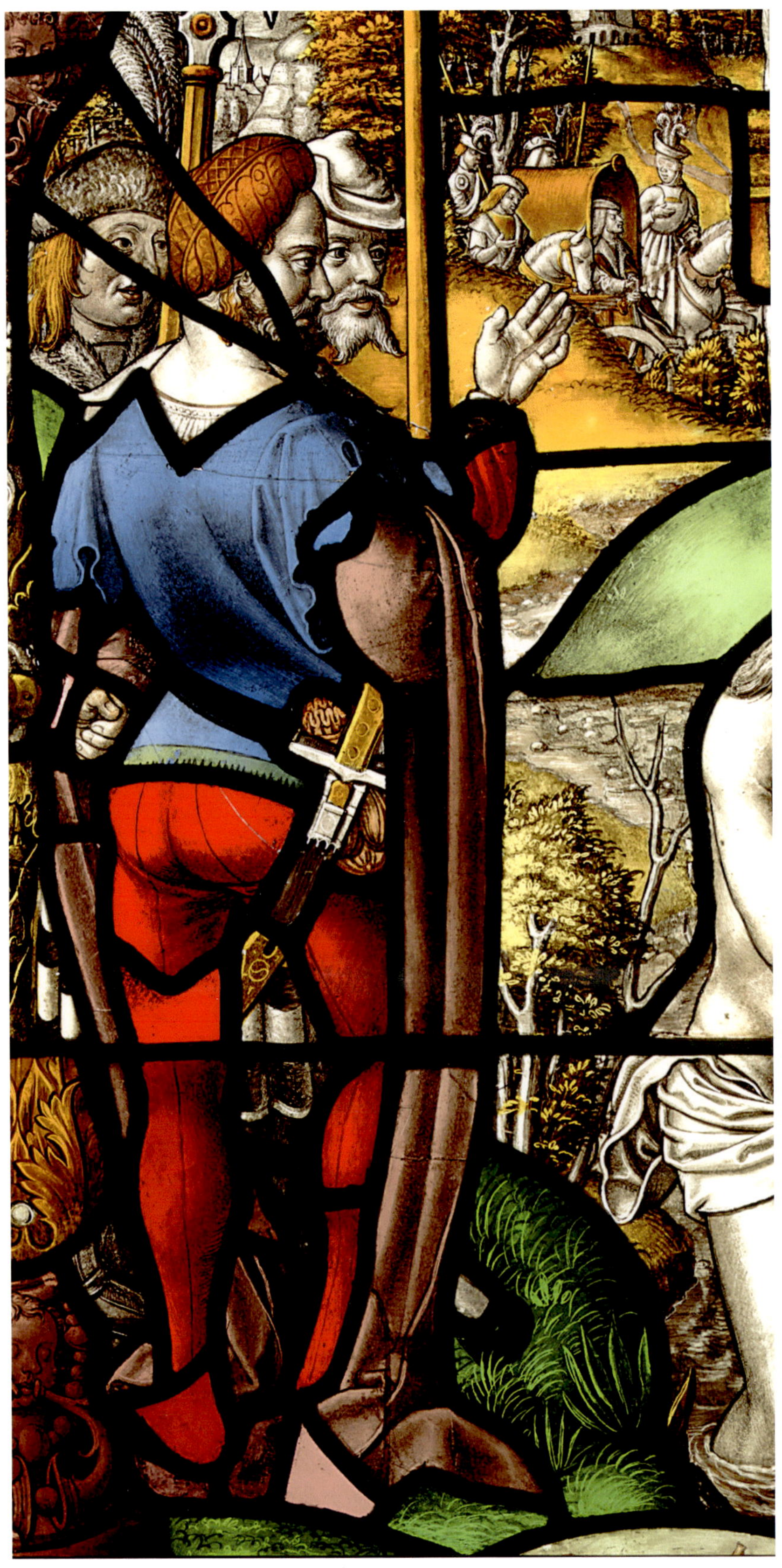

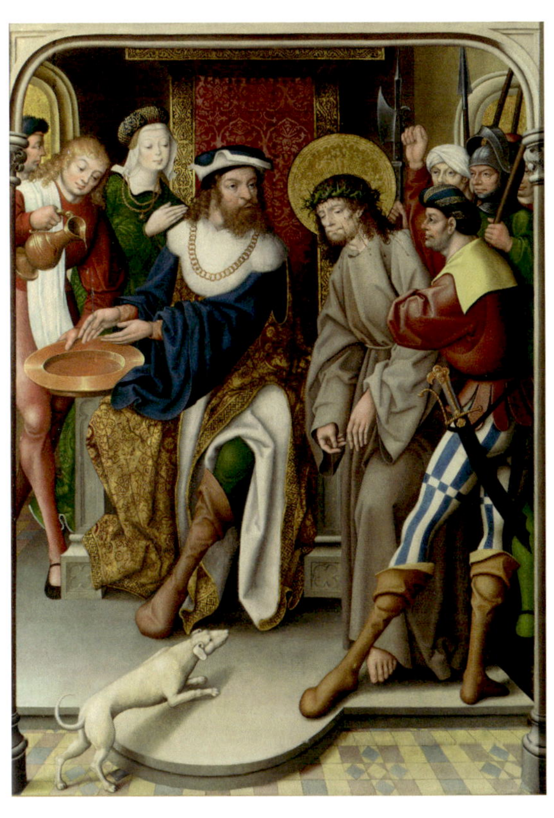

23 Master of Cappenberg (Jan Baegert?) (active about 1500–about 1525), *Christ before Pilate*, about 1520, oil on oak, 99.1 x 69.2 cm, The National Gallery, London

24 German, from the cloister of Mariawald Abbey, *The Presentation in the Temple*, about 1522–6, glass, 70 x 66.6 cm, V&A, London

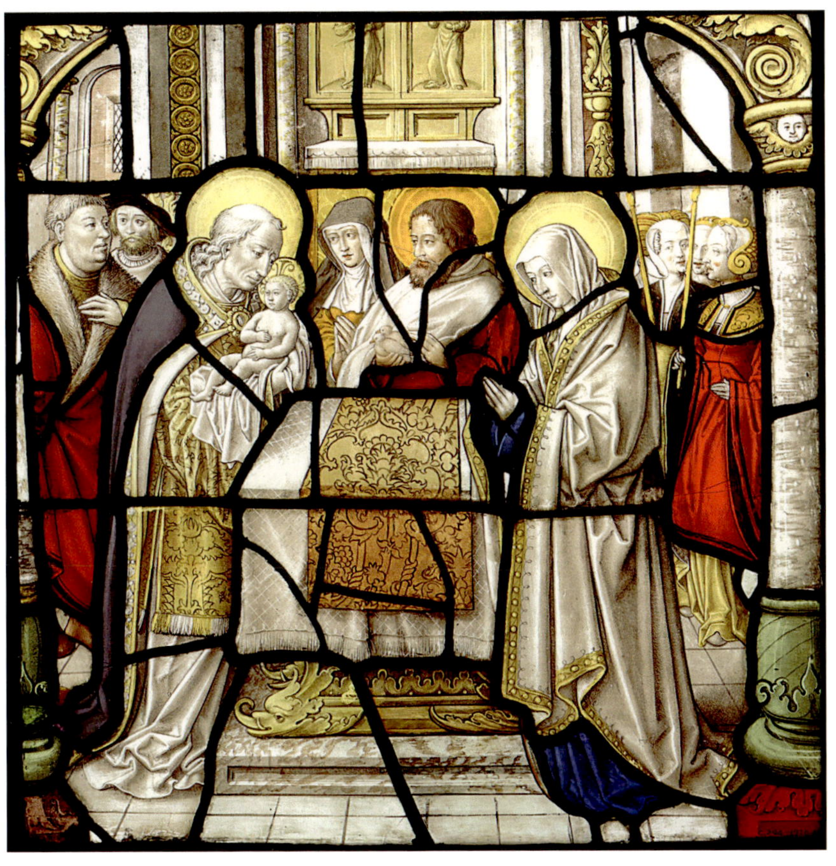

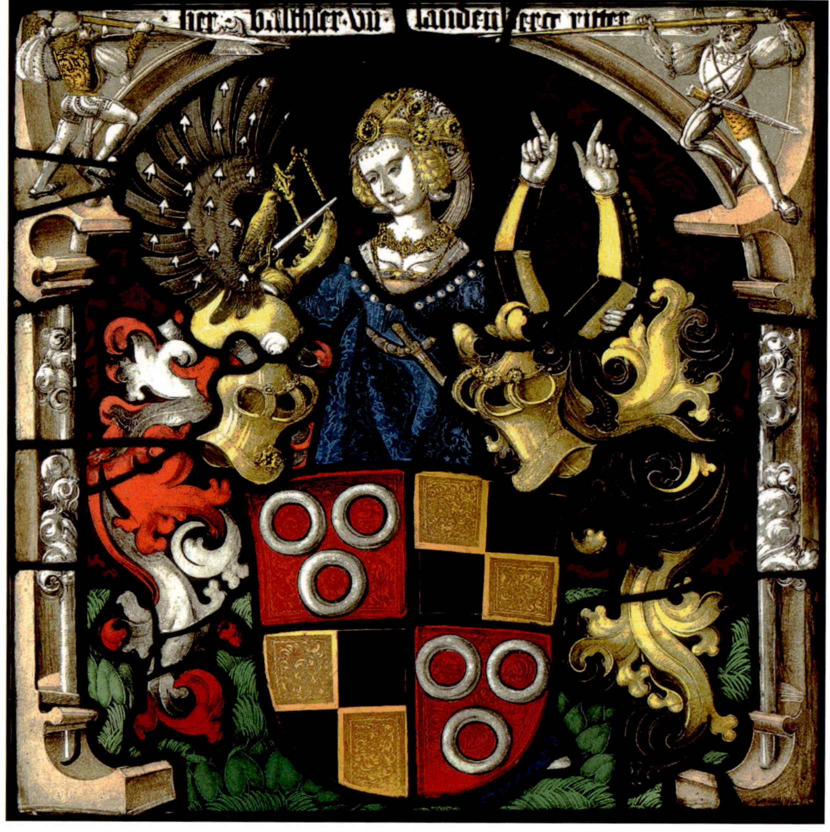

Glass was also employed for heraldry, which flourished in Renaissance Germany: in paintings, sculpted on tombs and depicted on glass. Its representation might offer considerably more scope to the glass artist than the simple symbolic shields seen in the window of the Liesborn *Annunciation* of about 1470–80 (fig. 27). A particularly elegant and lively example is that produced around 1500 by Lukas Zeiner, made to show off the coats of arms of Balthasar II von Hohenlandenberg (fig. 25). The design is arranged around the seductive, richly dressed female figure with her finely drawn, elaborately bejewelled headdress, and vivid blue damask dress, an effective foil to the deep plum design of the background. As heraldic supporter she languorously embraces the two chargers of Landenberg and Greifensee, while energetically battling men-at-arms rush from the spandrels. The dashing design shows off Balthasar's membership of the order of the fish and falcon, a knightly company to which he was admitted in 1492; the order is suspended from the crest of Landenberg, and the inscription reads 'Balthasar von Landenberg, knight'. The unidentified man in Baldung's portrait (fig. 26) also wears the order around his neck; he may be one of Baldung's patrons at the court of Baden in the Upper Rhine.

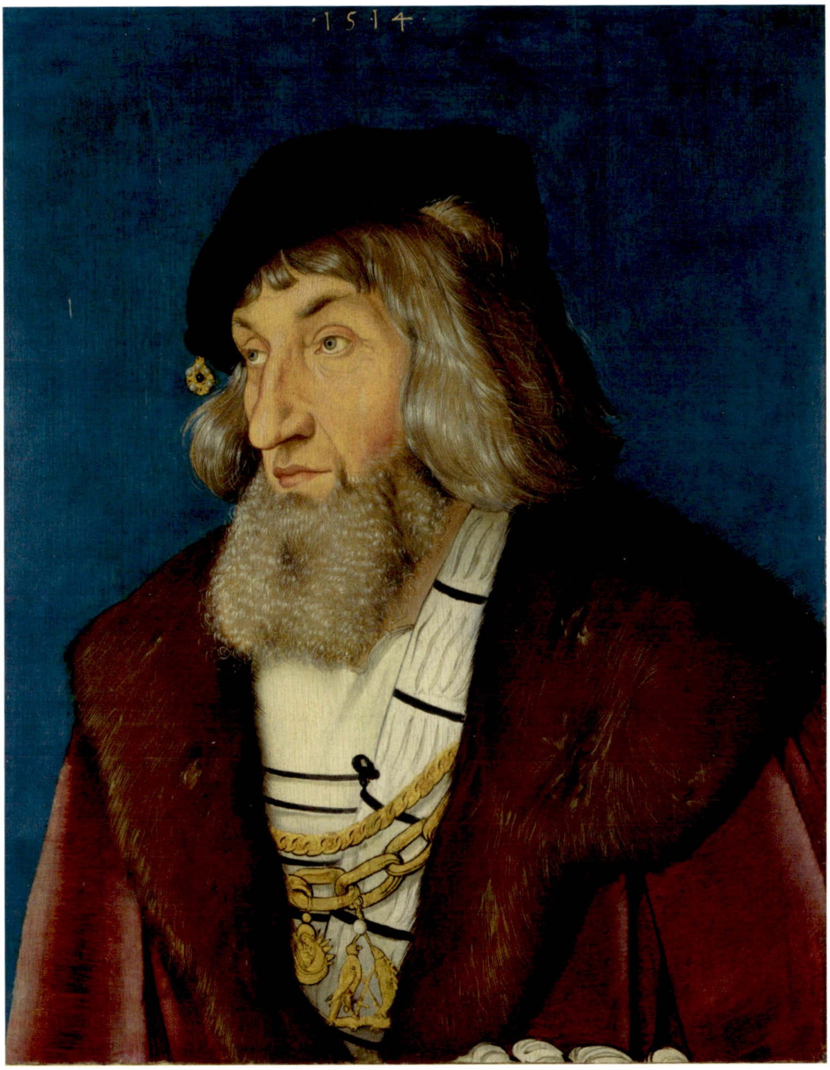

26 Hans Baldung
Grien (1485/5–1545),
Portrait of a Man,
1514, oil on lime,
59.3 x 48.9 cm,
The National Gallery,
London

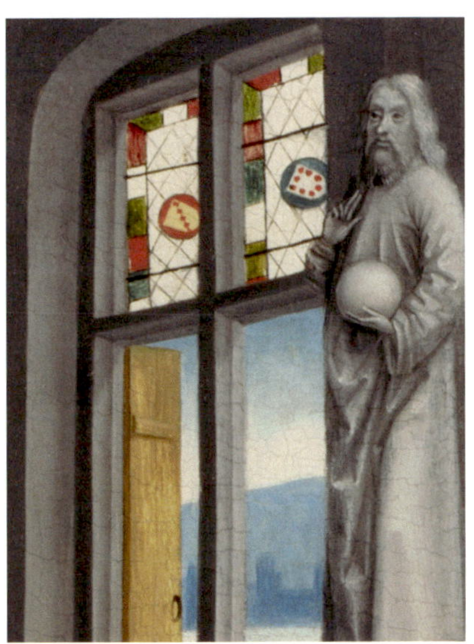

Small panels with a great range
of secular subjects, as well as
religious narratives and devotional
images such as the *Virgin as Queen
of Heaven* (fig. 11), were also
suited to windows in domestic
settings that were made up
predominantly from bulls' eye
glass. In contrast to the thicker
and more opaque bulls' eyes, these
panels were made from more
refined panes of glass, and so let
in more light. Jörg Breu won great
success producing designs for

27 Master of Liesborn
(active second half
of the 15th century),
detail from
The Annunciation,
probably 1470–80,
oil on oak,
The National Gallery,
London

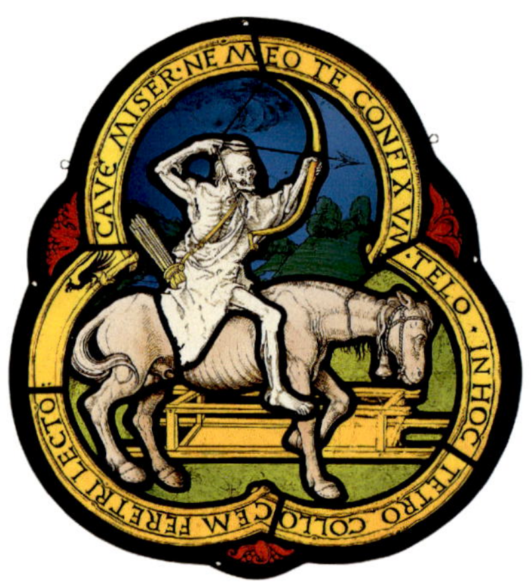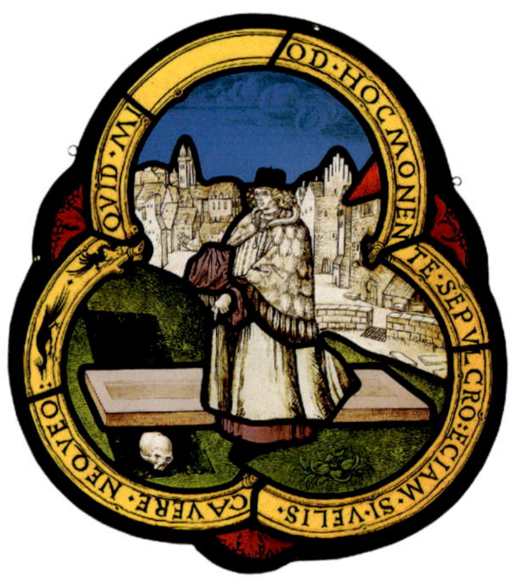

28 (left) *Death on Horseback taking Aim at Provost Dr Sixtus Tucher standing at his Open Grave*, 39.5 x 35.5 cm (MM 155) **29** (right) *Sixtus Tucher standing at his Open Grave*, 39.8 x 34.6 cm (MM 156)

series of small roundels, including classical subjects or the months of the year (figs 7 and 8), or, for the Emperor Maximilian's hunting lodge at Lermoos in the Tyrol, scenes of battles and hunting. *Coquinaria (The Art of Cooking)* (fig. 6) comes from a series of glass roundels illustrating trades including architecture, metalworking and making textiles, while Breu's drawing for *Ulysses and Telemachus* (fig. 8) probably derives from a series representing famous classical women such as Lucretia. Dürer produced two vivid small trefoil-shaped panels for the house of Sixtus Tucher, humanist theologian and diplomat, in Nuremberg in 1502 (figs 28 and 29). Tucher is shown before his grave, calmly meeting Death on horseback. Dürer did not entirely take account of the constraints of glassmaking in his design, which had to be adapted: the horse's mane could not be shown with projecting tufts of hair and the wooden bier was shortened so as not to interfere with its legs.

Dürer's and Baldung's work, as well as the Mariawald panels, represent the heights of the art of German Renaissance stained glass. After this date the Reformation antipathy to religious images meant that relatively little new glass was commissioned; in Nuremberg there was no new glass in churches after 1525. But it was not the Reformation which precipitated the removal of the paintings from Liesborn Abbey and the glass from Mariawald. It was the secularisation of German ecclesiastical foundations during the Napoleonic era in 1802 that resulted in their preservation in private collections and then in the National Gallery and the Victoria & Albert Museum respectively. This has happily enabled both paintings and the glass from Mariawald and other German foundations to be preserved and seen today so that the achievements of the art of German Renaissance glass can be fully appreciated.

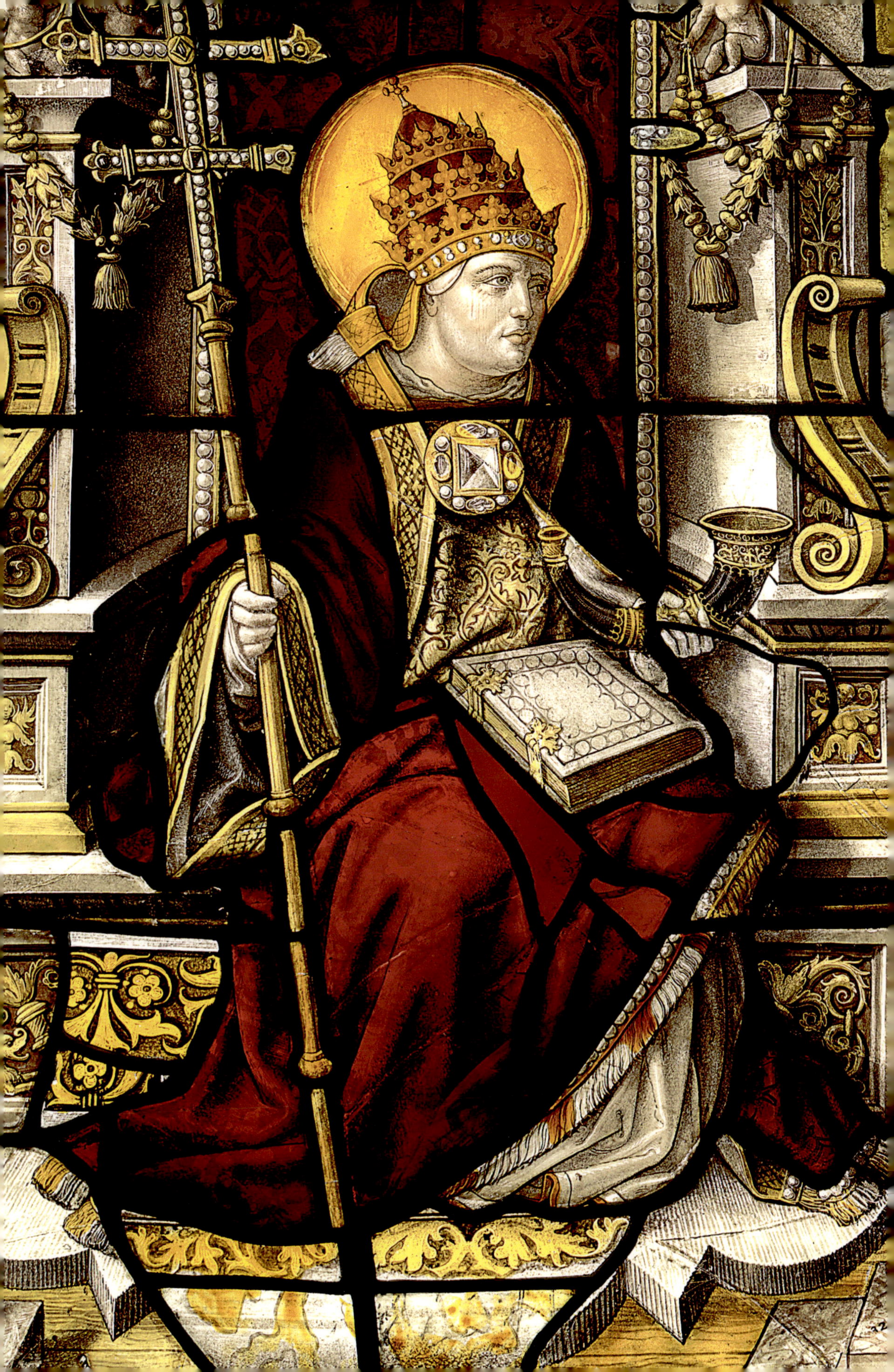

Further Reading

Sarah Brown and David O'Connor, *Medieval Craftsmen: Glass Painters*, British Museum, London 1991

Barbara Butts and Lee Hendrix, *Painting on Light: Drawings and Stained Glass in the Age of Dürer and Holbein*, exhibition catalogue, J. Paul Getty Museum, Los Angeles 2000

William Cole, *A Catalogue of Netherlandish and North European Roundels in Britain*, Oxford 1993

Timothy B. Husband, *The Luminous Image: Painted Glass Roundels in the Lowlands 1480–1560*, exhibition catalogue, Metropolitan Museum of Art, New York, 1995

Rainer Kahsnitz, 'Stained Glass in Nuremberg' in *Gothic and Renaissance Art in Nuremberg 1300–1550*, exhibition catalogue, Metropolitan Museum of Art, New York 1986, pp. 87–92

Andrew Morrall, *Jörg Breu the Elder: Art, Culture and Belief in Reformation Augsburg*, Aldershot 2001

Dagmar Täube (ed.), *Rheinische Glasmalerei. Meisterwerke der Renaissance*, 2 vols, exhibition catalogue, Schnütgen Museum, Cologne 2007

Theophilus, *On Divers Arts, the foremost Medieval Treatise on Painting, Glassmaking and Metalwork,* trans. John G. Hawthorne and Cyril Stanley Smith, New York 1979

Paul Williamson, *Medieval and Renaissance Stained Glass in the Victoria and Albert Museum*, V&A Publications, London 2003

See also the *Corpus Vitrearum Medii Aevi* website which includes images of the entire stained glass collection of the Victoria & Albert Museum: www.cvma.ac.uk

List of exhibits

Stained glass
Victoria & Albert Museum, London

Austrian (Styria)
The Annunciation to Saint Anne, about 1350–5 (fig. 5)
104 x 35.5 cm (C.72-1930)

German, after Jörg Breu the Elder
(about 1475–1537)
Coquinaria (The Art of Cooking), about 1520–30 (fig. 6)
23.5 cm diameter (604-1872)

German, after Jörg Breu the Elder?
Men drinking, 16th century
20.4 cm diameter (1236-1855)

The Virgin and Saint Anne (?), and the Healing of Saint Odilia, 1522
45.1 cm diameter (766-1907)

German, after Albrecht Dürer
(1471–1528)
The Flagellation, Ecce Homo (fig. 13) and
The Entombment, mid-16th century
64.7 x 93.5 x 2 cm (framed together)
(538-1907, 539-1907, 540 1907)

The Virgin as Queen of Heaven, about 1530 (fig. 11)
23.8 cm diameter (1237–1855)

German, from the cloister of Mariawald Abbey
About 1520–1 unless otherwise stated
The Prophet David (fig. 21a)
33 x 67.9 cm (C.236-1928)

The Prophet David (fig. 21b)
29.4 x 65.9 cm (C.239-1928)

Esau gives up his Birthright (figs 1 and 21c), 1521
69.6 x 67.3 cm (C.120-1945)

Naaman washing in the River Jordan
(figs 21d and 22)
69.6 x 65.9 cm (C.300-1928)

The Temptation of Christ (figs 9 and 21e)
71.5 x 70 cm (C.237-1928)

The Baptism of Christ (figs 2 and 21f)
73.2 x 66.3 cm (C.311-1928)

Saint Cornelius (figs 21g and 30)
77 x 70.5 cm (325-1982)

Abbot Heinrich von Binsfeld of Cornelimünster
(figs 10 and 21h) 77 x 70.5 cm (323-1928)

The Presentation in the Temple, about 1522–6
(fig. 24) 70 x 66.6 cm (C.294-1928)

German (Lower Rhine)
Tobias and Sarah on their Wedding Night, about 1520 (cover)
66 x 56.5 cm (C.219-1928)

German, from the cloister of the Abbey of Steinfeld, Gerhard Remisch?
(active to 1537–8)
Abbot Johann von Ahrweiler and Saint Norbert, about 1522
66.3 x 58.9 cm (C.270-1928)

Lukas Zeiner
(about 1450–1513)
The Arms of Balthasar II von Hohenlandenberg, about 1500 (figs 3 and 25)
50 x 48.5 cm (C.42-1919)

Paintings
The National Gallery, London

Austrian
The Trinity with Christ Crucified, about 1410 (fig. 4)
egg on silver fir, 118.1 x 114.9 cm (NG 3662).
Bought with a contribution from the Art Fund, 1922.

Hans Baldung Grien
(1484/5–1545)
The Trinity and Mystic Pietà, 1512 (figs 16 and 17)
Oil on oak, 112.3 x 89.1 cm (NG 1427)

Portrait of a Man, 1514 (fig. 26)
Oil on lime, 59.3 x 48.9 cm (NG 245)

Master of Cappenberg (Jan Baegert?)
(active about 1500–about 1525)
Christ before Pilate, about 1520 (fig. 23)
Oil on oak, 99.1 x 69.2 cm (NG 2154)

The Coronation of the Virgin, about 1520
Oil on oak, 97.2 x 70.5 cm (NG 263)

Master of Liesborn
(active second half of the 15th century)
Fragments from the Abbey of Liesborn,
probably 1470–80:
Head of Christ Crucified
Oil on oak, 32.7 x 29.8 cm (NG 259)

Saints Cosmas and Damian and the Virgin
Oil on canvas, transferred from oak
54.9 x 72.1 cm (NG 261)

Saints John the Evangelist, Scholastica and Benedict
Oil on canvas, transferred from oak
55.9 x 70.8 cm (NG 260)

The Adoration of the Kings
Oil on oak, 23.2 x 38.7 cm (NG 258)

The Annunciation (fig. 27)
Oil on oak, 98.7 x 70.5 cm (NG 256)

The Presentation in the Temple
Oil on canvas, transferred from oak
98.4 x 70.2 cm (NG 257)

Master of the Life of the Virgin
(active second half of the 15th century)
The Presentation in the Temple, probably
about 1460–75
Oil on oak, 83.8 x 108.6 cm (NG 706)

**Workshop of the Master of the
Life of the Virgin**
(active second half of the 15th century)
The Mass of Saint Hubert, probably 1480–5
Oil on canvas, transferred from wood,
123.2 x 83.2 cm (NG 253)

**Workshop of the Master of the Saint
Bartholomew Altarpiece**
(active about 1470–about 1510)
*The Virgin and Child in Glory with Saint James
the Great and Saint Cecilia*, about 1512
Oil on wood, 36 x 59.2 cm (NG 6497)

Prints and Drawings
The British Museum, unless otherwise stated

Hans Baldung Grien
(1485/5–1545)
*The Abbess Veronica von Andlau, with Nuns of
Cloister Hohenburg*, about 1510 (fig. 15)
Pen and brown ink on paper, 43 x 31.5 cm
Victoria & Albert Museum (D.199-1888)

Jörg Breu the Elder
(about 1475–1537)
March, before 1521 (fig. 7)
Pen and ink with wash on paper, 24.4 cm diameter
(1929-5-11-19)

Ulysses and Telemachus slaying the Suitors,
1522 (fig. 8)
Pen and ink on paper, 24.4 cm diameter
(1949-4-11-109)

Albrecht Dürer
(1471–1528)
Woodcuts, about 1497–1500
The Flagellation, 38.2 x 27.8 cm (E.3-79)
Ecce Homo (fig. 12), 39.2 x 28.4 cm (E.3-81)
The Entombment, 38.4 x 27.8 cm (1895-1-22-604)

Published to accompany the exhibition **The Art of Light: German Renaissance Stained Glass**
at The National Gallery, London from 7 November 2007 to 17 February 2008

The National Gallery thanks Apax Partners for their support

First published in Great Britain in 2007 by
National Gallery Company Limited
St Vincent House
30 Orange Street
London WC2H 7HH
www.nationalgallery.co.uk

ISBN 978 185709 348 3
525339

British Library Cataloguing-in-Publication Data
A catalogue record is available from the British Library

Project editors Jan Green and Davida Saunders
Designer Reena Kataria
Picture Researcher Maria Ranauro
Production Jane Hyne and Penny Le Tissier

Printed and bound in Hong Kong by
Printing Express Ltd